Colonial Kids

An Activity Guide to Life in the New World

Laurie Carlson

CHICAGO
REVIEW
PRESS

Library of Congress Cataloging-in-Publication Data
Carlson, Laurie M., 1952–
            Colonial kids : an activity guide to life in the New World /
    Laurie Carlson.
            p. cm.
    Includes bibliographical references.
    Summary: Gives instructions for preparing foods, making clothes,
and creating other items used by European settlers in America,
thereby providing a description of the daily life of these
colonists.
            ISBN 1-55652-322-X (alk. paper)
            1. United States—Social life and customs—To 1775—Activity
programs. 2. United States—History—Colonial period, ca.
1600–1775—Activity programs. 3. Children—United States—
History—17th century—Activity programs. 4. Children—United
States—History—18th century—Activity programs. [1. United
States—Social life and customs—To 1775. 2. United States—
History—Colonial period, ca. 1600–1775. 3. United States—
History—17th century. 4. United States—History—18th century.
5. Handicraft.] I. Title.
E162.C33 1997
973.2'071'2—dc21   97–13105
                                                                          CIP
                                                                          AC

CURR
E
162
.C33
1997

Published by Chicago Review Press, Incorporated
814 North Franklin Street
Chicago, Illinois 60610
ISBN 1-55652-322-X
Printed in the United States of America
5 4 3 2 1

For Dana, Caanan, Trelene, and Trevor; Rachel and Tom; Heidi; Curt, Liza, and Gretchen; Kendra and Atle—from your loving Aunt L.

Contents

Note to Readers

The term Native North Americans is used to represent those people who lived in America prior to European settlement. For brevity, when it is clear that the text is referring to one or more Native North American tribes, the term Indians is used to refer to all these people.

Time Line

1000
Norsemen land
at Vinland

1200
Greenland sagas
written down

1492
Columbus landed
in Caribbean

1504
Columbus made his
last voyage to
New World

1509
First African slaves
taken to New World
by Spanish settlers

1519
Spanish ships
took first horses
to New World

1608
French found
Quebec, Canada

1607
English found
Jamestown Colony

1598
Spanish found
Santa Fe

1570
Spanish settled at
Chesapeake Bay

1565
Spanish found
St. Augustine,
Florida

1620 Mayflower arrived
at Plymouth

1638
Swedish colonists
settled on Delaware River

1750
Population of
Europe = 140 million
Population of
Colonial America = 1½ million

1760
Russian fur traders
explored North
America's west coast

1776
American colonies
declared independence
from England

The People

What would you say if your parents told you they were taking you to an unknown land called the New World, where strange and unusual animals and plants lived? The trip would be made in a boat not much larger than a school bus. What if they mentioned there might be sea monsters, pirates, and, oh yes, worms in your food, during the sea voyage? And you would probably never be able to return to your homeland? Quite an adventure, wouldn't you agree?

A lot of children came to the New World and probably some of them really didn't want to. For most, though, the New World, and the opportunities that might be there were far better than where they had been living.

Look back into your own family's history—if they settled in North America before it became the nation it is today, they were *colonists*.

The North American colonies were settled by immigrants who came here and eventually formed their own countries—the United States of America, Canada, and Mexico.

There were people already here when the new-comers stepped off their ships. *Native North Americans* (North American Indians) already had built villages, even cities. They sometimes welcomed the new people, and sometimes fought them.

Native North Americans lived in villages all along the Atlantic coast when the European explorers arrived. Each Indian nation had its own territory, customs, style of dress, and language. The people hunted, fished, and planted gardens. They made things they needed out of wood, hide, bone, and shell.

Villages were usually small because too many people in one place would use up all the food. Many more people could survive in villages where gardens were planted.

Extra food was traded to other villages. People traded for items they couldn't gather or make. The Native North Americans depended on the land, the seasons, the weather, and on trading with each other for their survival.

Nations and villages sometimes fought each other over territory or trade—just like the European and Asian nations.

At the beginning of the colonial era in the New World, European explorers went everywhere they could looking for the most valuable things they

knew—gold, jewels, spices, even the fountain of youth.

They were able to travel because ship building and navigation had become refined and well developed. Ship building, map making, and charting the night sky made it possible for explorers to head across the ocean, looking for great riches.

The first colonists were soldiers who, in their search for riches found rich land instead. Soldiers from one country fought soldiers from other countries to claim the most land. Kings and queens were eager to snap up the biggest piece of the New World for their country and sent explorers and soldiers to do this for them.

The colonists that came after the explorers came to stay. They built towns and raised families. They wanted to live in a country where they could have freedom and opportunity—the very things they couldn't find in Europe.

Norsemen from ancient Scandinavia, led by Leif Ericson (a sailor from Greenland) were the first Europeans to land in North America. Ericson sailed in the summer of 1001 A.D. landing in eastern Canada and later exploring it. There they discovered a new plant, one they had never seen before—grapes. The men filled their boat with timber, grapes, and vines to take back to Greenland to show evidence of their discovery. In honor of this new discovery, they called this new land Vinland.

Sagas are stories or very long poems that were spoken aloud. Sagas told about the history of a family. Norsemen wrote down the saga of Erik the Red. That's one way people today learned about the Greenland colonies.

Why not use a notebook to write your own family's history—a family saga? You can start as far back as anyone remembers, and tell the story up to today. Try to write down all the obstacles and difficulties your family faced, and how they overcame them. Keep the notebook to pass on to your own children and grandchildren.

> **NOT ALL NORSEMEN were Vikings. Vikings were pirates who raided ships and villages, killing and stealing from others to gain their fortune.**

In 1492, Christopher Columbus set out from Spain with three ships, trying to find a sea route to Asia by going west across the Atlantic Ocean. Ten weeks later he came to an island, Hispaniola, and thought he had landed in India, so he called the natives he met *Indians*. He soon realized that he hadn't landed in Asia, so he made four more trips, from Spain, still searching for a route. On some voyages, his crew of 150 included about fifty twelve- and thirteen-year-old boys—that was one-third of his crew!

As soon as the news about Columbus's trips spread through Europe, other kings and queens sent ships and people to claim and settle the land for their own country.

Spanish colonists settled in southern Florida and the Caribbean Islands. Dutch colonists settled in what is now New York. Swedish colonists settled in what is now Pennsylvania. French ships carried settlers to the southeastern coast and into Canada. English ships brought most of the colonists who settled in New England and Virginia.

At first, most colonists were men and boys. In October 1608 the first two women arrived at James Fort. They quickly married two male settlers. Other women came and ten years later there were almost a hundred single women coming each year. They were

> **WHEN CHRISTOPHER COLUMBUS was young he read a book written by a man named Marco Polo who wrote about travel adventures in Asia. He dreamed of going to Asia someday, too, but Columbus wanted to go by ship. Read about Marco Polo's trip for yourself. After reading it, can you figure out why Columbus wanted to go by sea? Maybe you'll decide to be an explorer, too!**

Russian

Norse

English French

Spanish

WHAT DID COLUMBUS'S crew eat during their voyages? Kidney beans, salted fish, hardtack, dried fruit, vinegar, oil, and honey. Also, they ate garlic cloves to stay healthy.

auctioned off to men for marriage. James Fort was later called Jamestown, as it grew from a fort into a settlement.

In the Virginia colonies, an English child could pay for ship's passage by working as an indentured servant until he or she was twenty-one years old. An indentured servant was owned by his master and could be sold, traded, or gambled away. Orphaned children worked their way to the New World in order to have a free life outside of an orphanage.

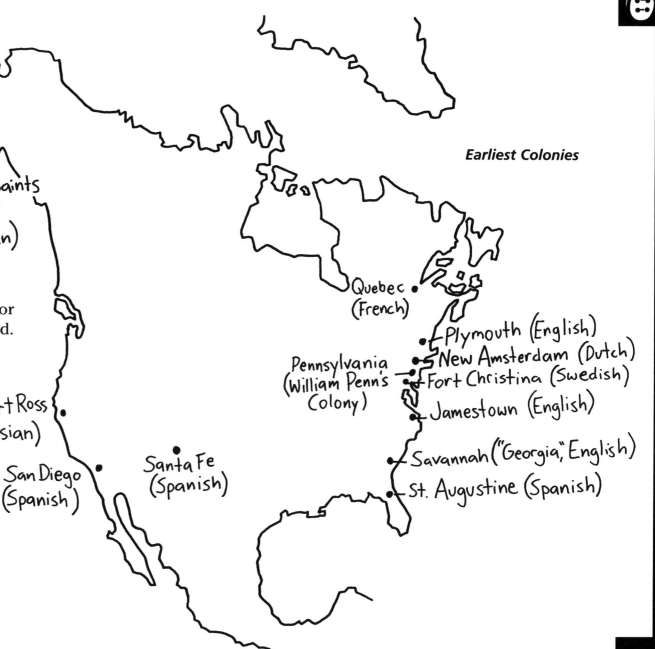

Earliest Colonies

Three Saints Bay (Russian)

Fort Ross (Russian)

San Diego (Spanish)

Santa Fe (Spanish)

Quebec (French)

Plymouth (English)
New Amsterdam (Dutch)
Pennsylvania (William Penn's Colony)
Fort Christina (Swedish)
Jamestown (English)

Savannah ("Georgia," English)

St. Augustine (Spanish)

Most newcomers expected to find some sort of riches in the New World. They thought there would be a lot of gold, and some ships were sent back to England full of fool's gold—actually rocks of pyrite that sparkled like gold but they were worthless.

Every citizen in England had to belong to the Church of England, which was headed by the King. A group of people who called themselves *separatists* wanted to form their own church because they didn't want to belong to the Church of England. They went to the Netherlands, but weren't happy living there because their children were learning Dutch ways and forgetting their English culture. The separatists decided to journey to the New World on a ship named the Mayflower. In exchange for passage and

THE OCEAN CROSSING was rough, but many people died while waiting on the ship to go ashore. On the Mayflower, eighteen women boarded the ship, only three were alive to get off; of twenty-eight children on the Mayflower, twenty-three survived; of the twenty-nine men and servants aboard, only ten were alive; and only fifteen of the thirty "Strangers" were alive to go ashore. It was a hard journey, and people had to fight off fever, scurvy, and pneumonia as well as cold weather to survive. By the following April when the Mayflower left to return to Europe, the village had only fifty colonists and half of them were children!

some supplies, the future colonists agreed to send back valuable goods for the merchants to sell in England. Their ship landed a hundred miles north of the Virginia colony. They built their own colony, called Plymouth, in what is now Massachusetts.

The Mayflower was overloaded with 102 passengers, but only 44 were really pilgrims or separatists who intended to stay in the New World. The rest were called Strangers by the pilgrims because they were recruited by merchants to join the venture.

Before the Pilgrims left the Mayflower they wrote up a set of rules to govern their new settlement. They didn't want the wealthy to rule; instead, they

Pilgrim means homeless traveler.

wanted every citizen to be equal with a government that represented everyone. It was a very new idea.

How were rule breakers punished? There were no police or sheriffs. There weren't any jails either because no one could take the time to build them with so much else to do. Lawbreakers were banished to the wilderness where they couldn't survive alone. Thieves were given a death sentence. Even swearing and complaining were quickly punished by whipping. It was important that everyone worked together so they would all survive. Crimes that endangered the colony were given the harshest punishment.

Because colonies were in danger from attack by other colonies or Native North Americans, it was important that all the men and boys trained as soldiers in case there was an attack. Villages had their own armies or *militias* for defense. Militias had been widespread in England. Any man who refused to train or fight was punished.

The Puritans were another group of people unhappy with the Church of England. They disagreed with the church's beliefs and thought the King should make the church's ceremonies less complicated. They wanted the ceremonies to be simplified and more Bible study. The Puritans came to North America and built a village called Boston in the Massachusetts Bay Colony.

> OTHER THAN A colony of Dutch at New Amsterdam (today's New York) and a colony of Swedes on the Delaware River, most people in the original thirteen colonies were from England. That's why they called it *New* England.

William Penn was an Englishman who adopted the Quaker religion. His father had loaned a lot of money to the King of England. To settle this debt, the King gave William a large piece of land in the New World where William began an experimental settlement. He created a colony called Pennsylvania, where all people would be equals. The rules were written up to be fair to everyone, even Native North Americans. It was a new idea.

The people who settled in Penn's colony were Quakers, a religion that teaches all people are equal. The Quaker colonists dressed plainly and called their church the Society of Friends. They came to the New World so they could practice their religion freely.

The last of the English colonies to be formed was Georgia. It was settled by many *debtors*—people who owed money to someone who they couldn't repay—who were released from debtors' prisons in England. They were sent to Georgia to raise silk worms and send all the silk back to England. In time, the settlers quarreled among themselves and turned to fur trading with the Native North Americans instead of silk farming. In a few years, most of the colonists had moved to other established colonies where they found better opportunities.

There were Russian colonies on the west coast of North America. Russian colonists settled at Three Saints Bay, near today's Kodiak, Alaska. They were busy trading metal items to Native North Americans in exchange for fur pelts that they shipped to China. Once there, Chinese merchants paid a good price for these furs. The Russian traders kept the fur trade a secret from other countries as long as they could so that they would be the only ones providing the Chinese with this precious good. Russian settlements, filled with traders, were built as far south as California.

At first, the New World colonies weren't very important to the rest of the world because little gold or riches were found. However, this changed when farmers began growing tobacco plants using seeds from the island of Trinidad. Tobacco sold for high prices in Europe. Tobacco farms were a way to make money, something the colonists needed. But tobacco farms needed workers because all the work—planting, hoeing, trimming, and drying— had to be done by hand. There weren't enough workers to hire because there weren't enough people in the colonies. In Europe and Asia, people had slaves to do these farming tasks, so farmers brought slaves and indentured servants to America to do this work. By 1700 there were more than a thousand ships bringing slaves from Africa to the colonies.

In 1705 there were four thousand black slaves and fourteen hundred Native North American slaves and indentured laborers working for four thousand English colonists. In the southern colonies, where more slave labor was needed on bigger farms, two out of every three people were enslaved. There were more slaves than free people.

IN THE EARLY 1600s the English colonies needed workers. Homeless adults and orphaned children were shipped to Virginia from London. The English thought this was a way to get rid of the poor and at the same time help the colonies.

Sailing and Settling

Everyone who came to the colonies in the New World had to come by ship. Some were large, with several levels for baggage, food, passengers, and animals. Others were really quite small—some the size of a school bus. The Norse, Spanish, and English ships were all powered by the wind. Large cloth sails caught the wind that pushed the ship across the ocean. The Norse had oarsmen, too, and their ships had flat bottoms, so they could travel through much shallower water, getting right up to the shore. The larger sailing ships had to stay anchored in deep water, and the people used smaller boats to row to shore.

There were 102 passengers on the Mayflower, 32 of them were children. It was ninety feet long—which is about the same length as two school buses.

HOW LONG DID a ship voyage last? That depended on how much wind was blowing. The first trips took up to eight months. Later, when the sea captains had better charts of the currents and winds, it took only about two-and-a-half months.

Build a Sailing Ship

fore

Glue the hull together at fore and aft.

aft

Fold the deck to shape.

Glue together and add a mast and paper sails.

Materials

White paper

Scissors

Brown construction paper or brown paper grocery bags

Glue

Drinking straw or coffee stir

Trace the 3 ship model pieces (2 sides and 1 deck) and cut out. Place these cut out pieces of paper on top of brown construction paper, then trace and cut out. Fold the flaps on the hull and glue these 2 pieces together. Next, fold the deck as shown and glue it to the completed hull. Cut out sails from the white paper. Use a pencil point to poke 2 holes in each sail and thread them through the straw. Poke a hole in the center of the ship's deck. Slide the straw through the holes. Now you have a sailing ship complete with a mast. Land ho!

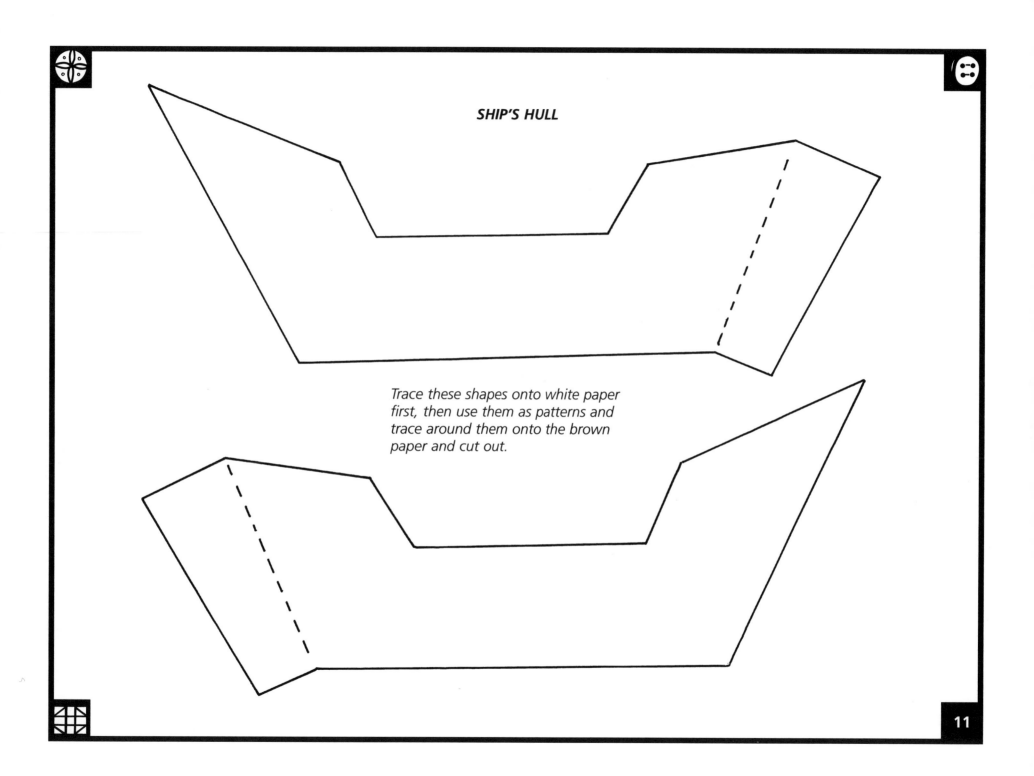

SHIP'S HULL

Trace these shapes onto white paper first, then use them as patterns and trace around them onto the brown paper and cut out.

SHIP'S DECK

apply glue here

glue

apply glue here

glue

glue

Fold on dotted lines as indicated.

SAILORS ATE HARDTACK. They were made of flour and water dough, baked, and dried until it was hard as a rock. It usually had worms in it. The sailors made a porridge of it and ate in the darkness so they wouldn't see the worms. There was sometimes meat on the ship, too. Every ship had a rat catcher, who gave his catch to the cook.

Sailor Stuff

Knots, Hitches, and Bends

Sailors had to know how to do many different tasks. Because the ship was powered by sails, it was very important that the ropes controlling the sails were in good shape and well-knotted. Everyone's life might depend on a securely tied knot.

Reef Knot: Also known as a square knot, this is the best known knot. You may already know how to tie it.

Bowline Knot: For hundreds of years, the bowline knot has been the most useful knot for sailors.

Clove Hitch: *Hitches* are used to tie the end of a rope to a post or dock. The clove hitch is the quickest to tie.

REEF KNOT

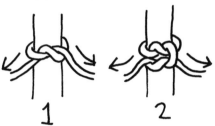

BOWLINE KNOT

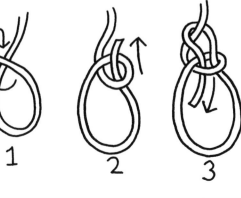

CLOVE HITCH

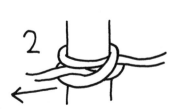

1. Wrap around post.
2. Overlap the rope.
3. Wrap it around the post again.
4. Bring around front and slip rope end under the second loop.
5. Pull end tight.

Sheet Bend: A *bend* is used to tie the ends of two ropes together. When a wild storm whipped up on the Atlantic, everyone on board hoped the sailors had tied the bends securely.

SHEET BEND

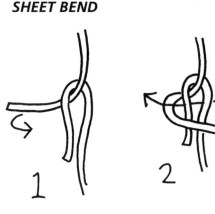

1. Wrap the rope ends together.
2. Slide one end behind the loop and pull out.

3. Pull the ends tight. A good knot to use for tying the ends of 2 ropes together to make a longer one.

Make a Darning Stitch

A sailor could never do his work "good enough." Everything had to be done the *right* way. It was important that every knot, splice, and stitch was properly done—a sailor's life and the lives of the rest of the crew might depend on it. Lives and the overall safety of the ship relied on every sailor's skills.

Cloth sails were cut and stitched by sail makers who spent years working as apprentices to older craftsmen. But on the seas, a sail could be torn during a storm and had to be stitched together immediately.

Thread for stitching canvas sails was rubbed with beeswax to make it strong and waterproof.

Metal needles had to be kept in cases made of bone or bamboo. If the needles got wet and rusted, they would crumble and fall apart. Then everyone on board was in trouble!

A small rip in a cloth sail could quickly be blown into a tear that could destroy a sail. Here's how to patch a small tear.

Materials

Large embroidery or crewel needle
Torn jeans or fabric scrap
Thread in a matching color
Scissors

Thread the needle with a doubled length of thread. Knot the ends together. Follow the drawing to stitch a tear closed. Pull the stitches smooth but not too tight, to just bring the edges of the torn fabric together.

Needle Hitching

Use this stitch to cover a water jug or bottle. Needle hitching was used to make covers for needle cases, knife holders, and tool handles.

Oarlocks were covered with hitching on whaling ships so they wouldn't make noise on a whale hunt.

Materials

Small jar

Yarn or thin cord

Large-eyed needle
(like a crewel needle)

Knot the end of the yarn around the rim of the jar.

Begin working stitches on the yarn tied on the rim. Loop loosely—don't pull the yarn tight.

Work stitches down the jar and across the bottom. Pull them tight as you move to the middle of the jar base.

Thread one end of the yarn through the needle. Wrap it around the top of the jar rim. Knot it and begin stitching the pattern. Work around and around until you cover the sides of the jar. Turn it over and keep going, doubling the stitches to pull it tight around the base of the jar. When you get to the end, cut the yarn and tie it in a knot. Tuck the end of the yarn up inside the hitching to hide it.

WITH NO FRESH food, sailors developed *scurvy*, a disease from lack of Vitamin C. On Vasco da Gama's first voyage to India, more than half his crew died of it. Sailors with scurvy had gums that swelled, flesh that dented easily, and wounds that didn't heal. They couldn't chew the hard food with swollen gums, so they starved, too. The cure? Fresh lemons, limes, potatoes, even vinegar and garlic cloves. People started calling the English sailors, "limeys."

Make a Compass

A ship's captain had to figure out where the ship was going to keep it on course. Ships traveled day and night, whenever the wind blew. At night he could study the stars and figure out what direction they were going. Daytime, he could use the sun for direction. What about when it was cloudy or stormy? Then he could use a compass.

We still use compasses to tell us where the four directions lie: north, south, east, and west. They are always in the same place, so we can tell where we are going if we know where one of the four directions lies.

Materials

Nail
Cork or piece of Styrofoam
Small magnet
Plastic or glass pan of water

Push the nail through the center of the cork. Make sure some of the nail sticks out both ends. Brush the nail across the magnet several times. Brush it in the same direction with each stroke. That will line up the electrons inside the nail, magnetizing it.

Drop the cork in a pan of water and watch what happens. It will float and bob a bit, then it will stop. The nail will point north. It lines itself up with the North Pole (a magnetic point on the earth).

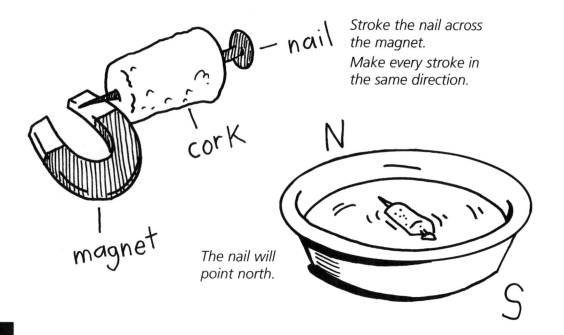

— nail

Stroke the nail across the magnet.
Make every stroke in the same direction.

cork

magnet

N

The nail will point north.

S

Dividing the New Lands

Who decided what country owned the seas and continents that were unexplored? After Columbus's first voyage, the Pope was asked to settle the question. In 1493, he drew a line straight down the Atlantic Ocean on a map of the world at the time. He gave all the new lands to the east of the line to Portugal (that was Africa) and all the lands to the west of the line to Spain (that was North and South America). Because Brazil juts out across the line, it was considered to be east of the line and went to Portugal.

This is how the unknown world was divided up. What do you suppose the French, Russians, Norsemen, and Native North Americans thought? How would you have divided it?

Fly a Flag

Early English colonial settlers flew the St. George flag. When King James of Scotland also became the King of England, he changed the flag to include the Scottish flag. The new flag was called the Union flag. When Jamestown was founded in 1607, the Union flag was flown there.

During the Revolutionary War, a flag with thirteen red and white stripes was used. The stripes meant the thirteen colonies were together and a snake across the stripes warned the English, "Don't tread on me."

The next flag to be used was called the Continental Colors. It had a small English flag in one corner, and thirteen red and white stripes. But after the Revolutionary War, Americans didn't want the new nation's flag to look like England's—after all, they had won independence.

VEXILLOLOGISTS CAN ANSWER your questions about flags. They study flags and flag history.

ST. GEORGE FLAG

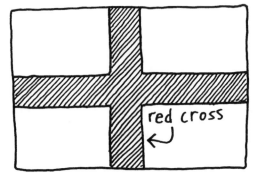

red cross

CONTINENTAL NAVY JACK

grey snake

13 red and white stripes

UNION FLAG, ALSO CALLED THE KING'S COLORS

white stripes red cross

blue background

A new flag was designed when the thirteen colonies joined to become the United States of America. It had thirteen red and white stripes and a blue patch in the top left corner covered with white stars, one for each state. It was years before the stars looked alike on every flag. For a long time, many flags had eight-pointed stars. Now, they're five-pointed stars called *mullets*.

Try drawing both kinds of stars. Which do you like best? Which is easier to make? Can you design others?

SHOW OUR NATION'S flag respect by following these rules:

Never put an object on it.

Don't let it touch the ground.

Never fly it upside down—that's a distress signal.

Fly a flag at half-mast only when someone has died.

Do be sure to fly the flag on Flag Day, June 14.

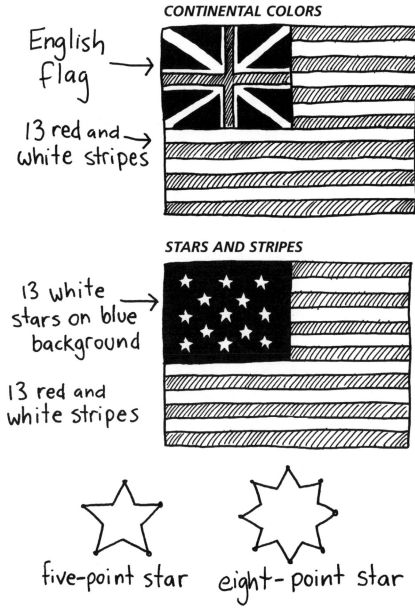

CONTINENTAL COLORS

English flag →

13 red and white stripes →

STARS AND STRIPES

13 white stars on blue background →

13 red and white stripes

five-point star   eight-point star

Clothes and More

Most colonists had only two sets of clothes. All clothing was made at home and took a lot of work to make. Wool was clipped from a sheep's back, then washed, dried, and colored with homemade plant dyes. (That meant gathering the plants and making the dyes, too.) Then the wool was dried again, carded (cleaned and untangled), spun into thread, then woven into cloth on a handmade loom. Once the cloth was woven it was cut up and sewn by hand into clothing.

People wore their clothes as long as they could until they really wore them out.

Clothing wasn't washed very often because the soap had to be made by hand, too. Soap was made from animal fat and wood ashes.

Up to age five or six, all children wore loose gowns. By age six they wore the same style of clothing as adults, or *upgrowns*, as they were called. When boys turned five or six they were given their first pair of *breeches* (trousers that end just below the knee). It was the age when children were given their first pair of real shoes, too. Before then, they went barefoot or wore slippers.

Boys' and Girls' Clothes

Boys' Clothes

Boys wore loose, long-sleeved shirts and pants. Their breeches were sometimes made of deer skin that stretched too big when they became wet, and shrunk too small when it dried. A vest was usually worn, too, and was made of deer skin or wool. Boys wore dark-colored, knitted socks that came up to their hips, worn beneath their pants. They always wore something on their heads, too, like wool knit caps or wide-brimmed hats.

PARENTS WERE ADVISED to make boys sleep without nightcaps to make them hardy. Also, parents wet their children's feet in cold water to make their feet tough.

Make a quick outfit for yourself. Wear a long-sleeved shirt, roll your pants up to your knees. Cut a *band* (collar) from white construction paper and tape it loosely around your neck. Make a vest from a brown grocery sack by cutting an opening along one full side, cutting holes for your arms, and cutting out a big circle at the bottom so your vest will rest on your shoulders. Find a knit cap to put on your head or cut a large sock in half to make one.

Girls' Clothes

Girls wore long dresses with tightly-laced belts, called *bodices*. Girls wore long aprons—a white cloth wrapped around their neck and shoulders and fastened with a pin—just like their mothers, and a cap on their heads.

To dress up like a colonial girl, make an apron from a pillowcase (see the following activity) and wear it over a long skirt. Tie a white cloth over your hair. Wrap and pin a white cloth (like a towel) around your neck and pin it in front.

For both boys and girls, cut large buckles from cardboard, cover them with aluminum foil, and tape or tie them onto the tops of your shoes.

Make an Apron

Materials

White or solid color pillowcase

1 piece wide-seam binding, 40-inches long, to match

Fabric glue (or stitch by hand or with a sewing machine with the help of an adult)

Match up centers of pillowcase and seam binding. Spread fabric glue inside binding. Fold over and press firmly to hold.

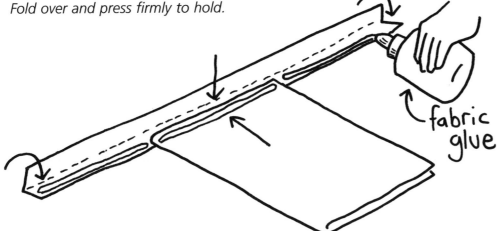

fabric glue

Fold the binding in half, lengthwise, to locate the center of the long strip. Then fold the binding widthwise. Fold the pillowcase lengthwise and place the shortest, seamed edge in the middle of the binding. (Match up the centers of the pillowcase and the binding so the binding will be the same length on each side.) Open the folded binding and apply fabric glue. Press the pillowcase in place, smoothly and evenly. Let dry. Apply glue to the other side of the pillowcase and binding and press down the binding. When dry, apply a thin line of glue down both inside edges of the binding, which will be used as the apron ties, and press down firmly. Wear your apron to protect your clothing when you do some cleaning or cooking, just like colonial women did.

Make a Wig

Wigs were very stylish in the colonies for many years. The style was brought over from Europe. Wig makers used human hair for the finest wigs. Cheaper wigs were made of horse hair, cow tails, goat hair, or thread.

Materials

1 pair of white hose or tights
Scissors
Rubber band
Plastic wrap
Polyester fiberfill quilt batting
Ruler
Craft glue
1 ribbon, 12- to 24-inches long

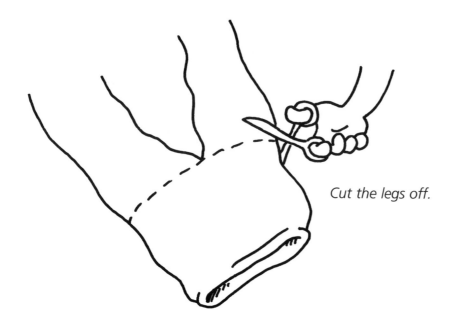

Cut the legs off.

Cut the legs off the tights and fasten the opening together with a rubber band. Turn inside out and place this on your head. Adjust the band until it fits, then remove the tights. Wrap plastic wrap over your hair (to protect it from the glue) and then place the tights back on your head.

Spread the batting on a table. Cut a piece about 12- by 24-inches.

Ask someone to help you glue the batting to the headpiece you made from the tights. Apply dots of glue on the headpiece along the front and center. Press the batting in place. Gently shape it when dry, by bringing the sides back and tying them in a ponytail with the ribbon.

Make curls out of the remaining batting by cutting long strips, rolling them up, and gluing them to the sides of the wig.

Can you imagine that even soldiers wore wigs under hats into battle?

NOT ONLY DID gentlemen wear wigs, but children, servants, prisoners, tailors, sailors, and soldiers wore them, too. By 1716, nearly everyone wore a wig. They were usually colored white or gray.

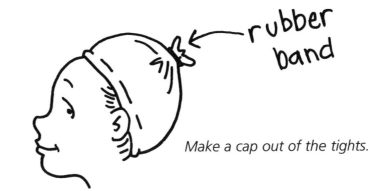

rubber band

Make a cap out of the tights.

Roll and glue the batting curls where you want them.

Glue the batting to the cap. Tie a ponytail in back.

Home Sweet Home

Colonial homes were simple. At first, people lived in tents made out of the ship's sails. They built *English wigwams* that were just like the Native North Americans' houses. They were made by bending young tree saplings into shape and pushing the ends into the ground to hold them in place. They covered the structure with brush, grass mats, and mud. When they had time, they sawed lumber and built houses like those in Europe.

Colonists had to make most of the items in their homes. There wasn't room on the ship to bring many possessions, and there were no stores to buy things from. Shopkeepers did set up small shops as soon as they could, but their goods were expensive.

A SWEDISH COLONY was started in the New World in 1638, and called New Sweden. The settlement was named Fort Christina, after the eleven-year-old queen of Sweden. Their goals were to get rich by trading for furs and gold with the Indians, but they had no luck. The settlement lasted only seventeen years.

DO YOU THINK all colonists lived in log cabins? In fact, none did, until 1642 when Swedish colonists along the Delaware River built houses like in their homeland. They built the walls out of logs, fitting them together and filling the cracks with mud and moss. It made a warmer house and was soon copied on the frontier.

Make a Rag Rug

By the time clothes finally wore out, about all they were good for was making rags. Since nothing was ever thrown away, colonial children were put to work making rugs from the old rags.

Materials

Strips of cloth, about 1-inch wide
(An old sheet is perfect.)

Fabric glue

Needle

Thread

Scissors

Large safety pin

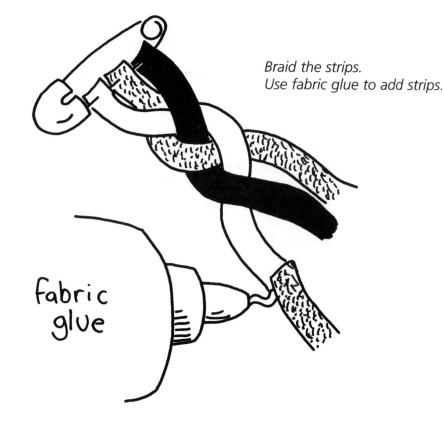

Braid the strips.
Use fabric glue to add strips.

fabric glue

You might want to make a small mat if you don't have enough time or many scraps. It could be used as a kitchen hot pad, as decoration under a plant pot, or as a mat for a favorite dog or cat to nap on.

You'll need three strips of cloth to begin braiding. Use a large safety pin to hold the ends together. You can slip this end into a drawer to hold it in place for easy braiding.

Start braiding: left side over, right side over left, and so on. Braid tightly, keeping the braid flat. Don't let it twist.

When a fabric strip ends, attach another with fabric glue and keep going. Continue to braid and glue on new strips. When you have a lot of braid to work with, begin sewing it into a rug.

Take out the safety pin and lay the braid on a table. Tightly coil the braid around itself, tucking the ends in and keeping it flat on the table. Use a needle and thread to sew the braid together. Start stitching in the center, and work toward the outside edge as you continue coiling the braid.

When you get to the end of the braid, tuck the strips inside the coil and stitch over the ends to hide them.

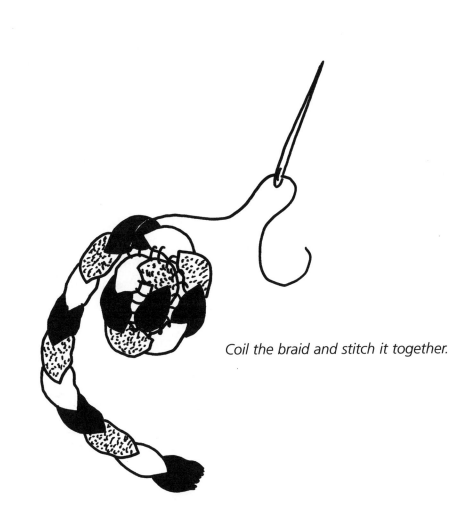

Coil the braid and stitch it together.

Paint a Chest

Chests were found in nearly every room in colonial homes. No one built closets in their houses, in part, because closets were counted as rooms and houses were taxed by the number of rooms they contained.

Chests held clothing, blankets, towels, sheets—anything that had to be stored away.

People brought chests to hold their few belongings aboard ship and later used these same chests in place of chairs and tables until they were able to build furniture.

The brightest painted chests were made by Pennsylvania Dutch craftsmen, who were actually from Germany.

Popular designs were hearts, flowers, birds, and shapes and patterns in circles.

Materials
Cardboard or wooden box with lid
Tempera or acrylic paints
Pencil
Black fine-tip permanent marker
Paint brushes

Paint the box a light color. When it's dry, use the pencil to draw some of these German designs or make up some of your own. Trace over the pencil lines with a black fine-tip permanent marker. Fill in the designs with bright colors of paint. You can use this decorative box to store your valuables like baseball cards, pictures of family and friends, or some other keepsake.

Paint a Cloth Rug

Rich people bought carpets made in England or the Orient, but most colonists couldn't afford them. Instead, rugs made of canvas (like a ship's sails) were painted bright colors.

Materials

1 piece off-white, light-tan canvas or denim, 18 by 36-inches

Scissors

Newspapers

Acrylic paint

Paper plate

Sponges cut in design shapes (like hearts, stars, or tulips)

Spray bottle of clear acrylic sealer

Fray all four sides of your piece of canvas or denim by pulling threads out until you have about ¼ inch of fringe on each side.

Put newspapers on the floor or other flat surface to catch any paint that might soak through the fabric. Lay the rug on top of the newspapers.

Pour some paint onto the paper plate. Wet the sponge in water and squeeze it so it's just damp. Press the design edge of the sponge into the paint, then gently press it on top of the rug. Keep decorating the rug with these designs until you're satisfied with how it looks.

Let it dry completely, then spray it with acrylic sealer to protect the design.

It's a perfect little rug to put beside your bed.

Silver Plate a Tray

Silversmiths made candlesticks, platters, bowls, and eating utensils. Silversmiths could make intricate decorations by *engraving* (cutting designs with a sharp tool) on the metal.

Almost every town had a silversmith. The most famous silversmith was Paul Revere. When he was a teen he already had become known for his carefully made silver bowls, pitchers, and tea sets. His father (who was also a silversmith) taught him the craft. You might already know Paul Revere as the man who, at the start of the Revolutionary War, rode through the night warning that English troops were approaching.

Materials

White glue
Paper plate
Scissors
String
Styrofoam tray
Aluminum foil
Toothpick

Dip pieces of string into the glue and arrange it on the tray.

string

glue

Squirt some glue onto the paper plate. Dip pieces of string in the glue and arrange it on the Styrofoam tray to make a design. Let it dry. Cover the tray with aluminum foil, pressing it gently over the string so the design shows up. Glue the edges of the foil at the back of the tray. Use the toothpick to gently engrave (press) a design in the foil.

PAUL REVERE ALSO made false teeth out of gold. He advertised in the town newspaper. Today people still get gold crowns made by dentists.

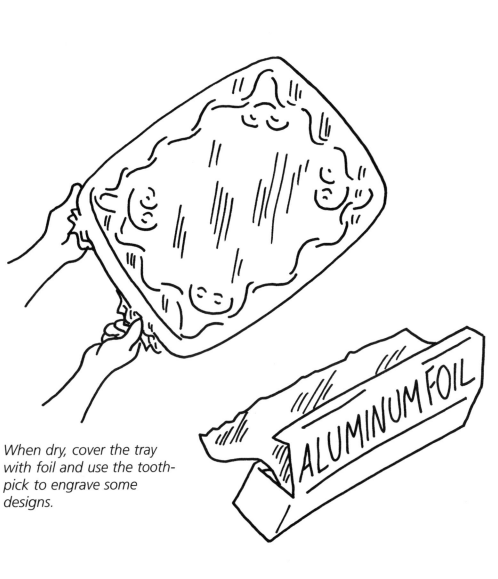

When dry, cover the tray with foil and use the tooth-pick to engrave some designs.

Dinnertime!

olonial meals were simple. There weren't many foods to choose from, and not many ways to cook things. There were no cooking stoves, so everything was cooked over the fireplace. Some people sent to England for metal boxes that breads and pies could be baked in. These were called *ovens* and were set in the fireplace to heat.

Children did a lot of the gathering and preparing of foods. Children were given the jobs of stirring the stew or turning the roast over the fire. They churned butter, hulled corn, and cracked nuts. Six-year-olds were expected to work diligently and older children were given the same work as adults.

Churn Butter

The Mayflower Pilgrims and other early colonists didn't have fresh butter—they didn't have any cows. In 1624, Dutch colonists brought livestock in three specially made ships, named for their cargo: the *Sheep*, the *Cow*, and the *Horse*. When cows were brought by ship they were valuable and treated *very* well. As years passed, herds grew, until nearly every family had a cow for milk and cream. Then everyone could make their own butter and cheese.

Colonial children made butter in wooden buckets called *churns*. They turned a wooden paddle inside the churn which stirred the cream.

¼ pound butter (@1 butter stick)

Butter was made by turning a wooden paddle in a wooden churn.

Ingredients
½ pint whipping cream
Crackers

Utensils
Glass jar with tight-fitting lid
(such as a mayonnaise jar)

Fill the jar a half or a third full of cream. If you use baby food jars, divide the cream into 3 jars (and get some friends to join in).

Screw the lid on tight and begin shaking the jar. Keep shaking it back and forth until the cream thickens, and then turns into butter. It will turn into a solid yellow ball, and the thin buttermilk will separate from it. It will take less than 10 minutes for the butter to form.

Shape the butter into a round ball or press it into a fancy shape with a cookie cutter. Colonists used wooden butter molds to make a design on cakes of butter.

Spread the butter on crackers and enjoy!

Be sure to store any leftover butter in the refrigerator.

You can shake the whipping cream in a jar.

Corn Bread

Aboard ship, travelers ate bread made from flour and water, baked hard, called hardtack. It would last for years. It tasted terrible, but kept people from starving to death. Once they were in the New World, colonists were quick to try making foods that tasted better.

Colonists had never seen a plant like corn, but the Native North Americans had been growing it for seven thousand years in many areas of the New World. They called it *maize* (say it: mayz).

Corn was dried and the kernels ground into cornmeal for bread. The husks were fed to the pigs, burned in the fireplace for warmth, or used to stuff mattresses.

8 to 16 servings

CORN IS A PLANT that can't reseed itself. It must always be seeded by a person. Wild corn has never been found.

Ingredients

1 cup yellow cornmeal

½ cup flour

¾ teaspoon salt

1 cup milk

1 egg

2 tablespoons vegetable oil

Butter or molasses

Utensils

Mixing bowl

Measuring cups

Measuring spoons

Spoon

1 8 by 8-inch baking pan, greased

(Adult help suggested.) Preheat oven to 425° F. Mix the cornmeal, flour, and salt in the bowl. Stir in the milk, egg, and oil. Beat until it's a smooth batter. Pour into the greased pan. Bake at 425° F for 15 minutes. Cut into pieces and eat it while it's warm with butter or molasses.

Trenchers

Early colonists didn't have dinner plates. They ate from *trenchers* that were squares of wood with a hollow spot carved in the center. Two children or a husband and wife shared one trencher at meals. Really elegant homes had a trencher for each person to use. At Harvard College, wooden trenchers were bought by the gross (a dozen dozen) for students' meals.

Some families used a *tableboard*, which was a wooden tabletop with hollowed-out spots for food. The whole tabletop was washed after a meal.

Trenchers were pieces of hollowed-out wood that served as plates. People shared them.

Hasty Pudding

Colonists ate a lot of puddings. They weren't like the milk puddings we enjoy today because milk was so scarce. Puddings were cooked porridge, only a bit thicker. Leftover pudding was saved. For breakfast, people sliced the thickened leftover pudding and fried it or baked it.

7 servings

Ingredients

1 cup yellow cornmeal

4 cups water, cold

½ teaspoon salt

Butter or margarine

Maple syrup, brown sugar, or molasses

Utensils

Mixing bowl

Measuring cup

Measuring spoons

Saucepan

Spoon

(Adult help suggested.)
Mix the cornmeal and 1 cup of cold water in a bowl. Put 3 cups of water in a saucepan and add ½ teaspoon of salt. Heat it to boiling. Slowly stir in the cornmeal mixture. Cook on low heat for 15 minutes, stirring often to prevent lumps from forming. Serve it warm with a pat of butter and a dash of maple syrup, brown sugar, or molasses.

IF IT HADN'T been for the Native North Americans' corn, the first English colonists might have starved to death. The colonists wanted to grow mulberry trees as food for silkworms, in order to make money through trade. The governor had to make it the law that everyone plant some corn so that they could feed themselves in future seasons.

Gingersnaps

Spices are the reason the New World was discovered by Columbus. Spices were so important to Europeans that merchants decided to go get them from Asians themselves. They wanted to break the monopoly the middlemen—the Italians, Mongols, Arabs, and Turks—had over the spice trade. In the process of trying to find a short route to Asian spice markets, Columbus landed in the New World.

This spicy cookie recipe uses many of the favorite spices these explorers were seeking.

4 dozen cookies

Ingredients

1 cup brown sugar, firmly packed

¾ cup shortening

2 tablespoons molasses

1 egg

2½ cups flour

2 teaspoons baking soda

¼ teaspoon salt

1 teaspoon ground cinnamon

1 teaspoon ground ginger

½ teaspoon ground cloves

Granulated sugar

Utensils

Mixing bowl

Measuring cup

Measuring spoons

Spoon

Baking sheet, greased with shortening

(Adult help suggested.) Preheat oven to 375° F. Mix the brown sugar, shortening, molasses, and egg together. Stir in the flour, baking soda, salt, and spices. Shape the dough into balls, about the size of egg yolks. Roll each ball in sugar. Place the balls about 3 inches apart on a greased baking sheet. Bake them for 10 minutes.

VASCO DA GAMA, a Portuguese captain, *did* find the first route to India. When the Portuguese took over the spice trade they raised prices even higher.

Pound Cake

This recipe (called a *receipt* in colonial times) for pound cake was easy to remember. Can you figure out why?

3 loaves

Ingredients

1 pound butter or margarine (4 sticks)

1 pound sugar (2 cups)

1 pound flour (3¼ cups)

1 pound eggs (that's 8 large eggs)

½ cup water

1 tablespoon vanilla

Utensils

Mixing bowl

Measuring cup

Spoon

3 bread loaf pans, greased with shortening

(Adult help suggested.) Let the butter sit at room temperature until it's soft. (Or, put it in the microwave for 10 seconds to soften it.) Preheat the oven to 325° F.

Stir all the ingredients together. Pour the batter into the greased pans. Bake for 1 hour.

Spiced Cider

WHAT ABOUT TEA? In the early years of the colonies, tea was too expensive. Also, people didn't seem to know how to consume it. When it was first sold in Massachusetts, people boiled the tea leaves, poured off the water, and ate the leaves with butter and salt. Not surprisingly, they weren't very impressed with the taste of tea.

When the Revolutionary War started, patriots dumped tea in Boston Harbor to protest the high English taxes levied on it. People drank herb tea instead and called it *liberty tea*.

Colonists didn't drink very much water because their drinking water was unclean and made them sick. Their wells were dug with shovels and they had no sewers, so bacteria thrived in the drinking water. They drank beer, rum, cider, wine, and milk (once there were enough cows).

Here's an easy way to make a delicious spiced drink. It's great for Halloween, New Year's Eve, or any cold night.

1 gallon

apple cider

cloves

cinnamon sticks

Ingredients

1 gallon of apple cider
A few whole cloves
2 or 3 cinnamon sticks

Utensils

Large saucepan or pot
Ladle
Drinking mugs

 (Adult help suggested.) Pour the cider into a saucepan or pot. Drop the cloves and cinnamon sticks in the saucepan and heat it, over a low setting, until it's very warm, but not boiling. Use the ladle to pour the cider into mugs. Be sure to let it cool before enjoying.

If you want to prepare the cider in the microwave, sprinkle a dash of ground cinnamon and ground cloves in each mug of cider. Stir, then heat for 1½ minutes on high.

Baked Apples

Colonists brought apple seeds with them on ships and planted orchards right away. Whenever anyone ate fresh fruit they saved the seeds for planting more trees.

4 baked apples

Trim the top and scoop out the core.

Ingredients

4 large apples
¼ cup brown sugar
1 tablespoon ground cinnamon
Butter or margarine
¾ cup hot water
2 tablespoons sugar

Utensils

Paring knife
Spoon or vegetable paring tool
Measuring cup
Measuring spoons
1 8 by 8-inch baking pan

(Adult help suggested.) Preheat oven to 375° F. Wash the apples and cut out the core. Use a knife and spoon to scoop out the center, or better yet, use a vegetable paring tool. Don't cut through the bottom of the apple. Trim the peel away around the top.

Spoon brown sugar into the center hole of each apple. Sprinkle cinnamon in the centers, too. Put a thin slice of butter on top of each apple's center.

Put the apples in the baking pan and pour the hot water in the bottom of the pan.

Bake for 1 hour. (Small apples may not take as long to cook.) Apples are done when an inserted knife goes in smoothly.

COLONISTS HAD TO store food for winter. They didn't have refrigerators or freezers, and canned food hadn't been invented yet. They saved food by drying it, like the Native North Americans did.

Fill the apples with brown sugar and cinnamon.

Candied Orange Peel

Colonial kids didn't have many sweet treats to enjoy. Sugar was expensive and hard to come by. In those days, candied treats were called *sweet meats.*

Here's one candy treat that children long ago might have looked forward to. After enjoying a very special treat—an orange—kids waited for their mother to make candy from the peel. Nothing went to waste in the colonies!

2 cups

Ingredients

3 oranges

Water

1 tablespoon salt

2 cups sugar

Sugar, to roll peels in

Utensils

Large bowl

Measuring spoons

Plate or medium bowl

Colander

Spoon

Knife (plastic serrated knife will work)

Saucepan

Measuring cup

Waxed paper

(Adult help suggested.) Wash the orange skins, then peel them carefully. Try to keep the peels in long strips. (Eat and enjoy the oranges!)

Place the peels in a large bowl. Add enough water to cover them and the salt. Set a plate or smaller bowl on top the peels to hold them under water. Let them soak overnight. (This will take out the bitter taste.)

Drain the salt water off and rinse the peels in fresh water. If the peels have thick white membrane, scrape it off with a spoon.

Place the peels in a saucepan and cover with water. Heat to a boil. Cook for 20 minutes. Drain the hot water off and cover the peels with fresh water. Boil and drain again. Let the peels cool.

Cut the peels into strips about as wide as a pencil.

Place the peels in the saucepan. Add ¾ cup water and 2 cups sugar. Stir and cook slowly over low heat for 30 minutes, until the water has cooked away.

Let cool. Roll the strips in sugar, and lay them on waxed paper to dry. You can make candy from grapefruit and lemon peels, too.

THE SUGAR STORY

Spanish settlers began growing sugarcane on islands in the Caribbean. They needed workers. In Europe, people had slaves to do the work. In Spain, rich families owned at least fifty slaves. So, they looked for slaves. The Portuguese colonists were growing sugarcane in Brazil and they began buying and selling slaves. At first they captured Native Americans and made them slaves. Soon the number of free Native Americans dwindled. That's when the Spanish settlers looked to Africa for additional slave labor where traders were quick to sell captured people to the sugar farmers.

Sugar was so important that the Dutch traded their New York colony to England in exchange for the sugar lands of Surinam (a country in South America, then known as Dutch Guiana). France abandoned Canada to the English for the sake of Guadeloupe, a sugar growing island in the West Indies.

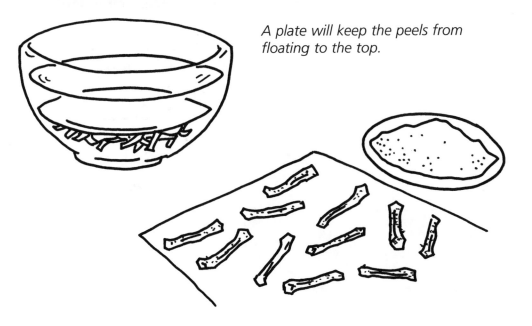

A plate will keep the peels from floating to the top.

Steamed Clams

Colonists in New England found Native North Americans gathering and baking a strange food—clams. Most of the colonists hadn't eaten them before. The Native North Americans baked theirs in fire pits in the ground. Colonists cooked theirs in the fireplace. You can cook yours on a stove top or hot plate.

10 clams

CLAM SHELL SPOONS

Colonists had wooden or pewter spoons, but some also made clam shell spoons. Save your clam shells to try it. Use a stick about six-inches long. Have an adult slit one end with a pocket knife. Slide a clam shell into the slit. Wrap with tape.

Clam shell spoons were good because they didn't have to be polished every week, like pewter. Because of their flat shape they were useful to skim cream off buckets of fresh milk.

Ingredients

½ pound fresh clams, in the shells (10 clams)

Cold water

Salt and pepper to taste

Butter

Utensils

Large pot with lid

Measuring cup

Tongs

Soup bowl

Fork

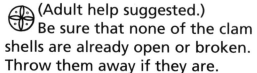

(Adult help suggested.)

Be sure that none of the clam shells are already open or broken. Throw them away if they are.

Rinse the clams and put them in the pot. Add ½ cup cold water. Put a lid on the pot and heat on medium-low for 10 minutes or until all the shells open up. Use tongs to place them in a bowl. They're ready to eat!

If a clam shell won't open during cooking, it's spoiled—don't eat it.

To eat the clams, pry the shells open with a fork and scoop the meat out with the fork or use your fingers. Sprinkle with salt and pepper and dip in melted butter if you like.

Clam Chowder

Chowder was very popular because a pot could be kept cooking over the fireplace all day. People could serve themselves whenever they were hungry, and more ingredients could be added to the pot for the next day. It was a good, hot meal and gave the cook a chance to get other work done.

6 servings

Ingredients

4 large potatoes

2 cups water

1 tablespoon dried onion flakes

¼ teaspoon ground thyme

½ teaspoon salt

1 6-ounce can minced clams

2½ cups milk

2 tablespoons flour

2 tablespoons bacon bits

Utensils

Peeler

Knife

Cutting board

Measuring cup

Measuring spoons

Large pot with lid

Spoon

Ladle

Small serving bowls

(Adult help suggested.)
Peel the potatoes and cut them in cubes the size of dice or about 1-inch square.

Stir into a pot 2 cups water, the potato cubes, onion flakes, thyme, and salt. Put on the lid and simmer 15 minutes. Stir in the clams and 2 cups milk.

Put ½ cup milk and 2 tablespoons flour in a small bowl. Stir until it's smooth. Try to mash out any lumps. Add this paste to the soup.

Stir and cook the chowder a few minutes longer. It will get thicker as it cooks. Sprinkle with bacon bits before serving.

WANT TO TRY eating chowder the old fashioned way? You'll need a small, round loaf of bread. Use a spoon to cut off the top and scoop out most of the soft bread but leave the bottom in place. Put the bread bowl on a plate and fill with thick chowder. Eat the bowl and all!

Cut off the top and scoop out the center.

Fill with hot chowder. Yum!

Pumpkin Pie

For many colonists, pumpkins were the difference between survival and starvation. Native North Americans grew them and traded or sold them to the colonists until the colonists had saved up pumpkin seeds and learned to plant their own.

People ate pumpkin soup, pumpkin pudding, baked pumpkin, boiled pumpkin, pumpkin pancakes, and, of course, pumpkin pie. People jokingly called Thanksgiving Day, St. Pompion's Day. (Colonists spelled pumpkin, *pompion*.)

You might want to make your pumpkin pie like colonists did—in a square pan.

Here's an easy way to enjoy the versatile pumpkin.

1 pie

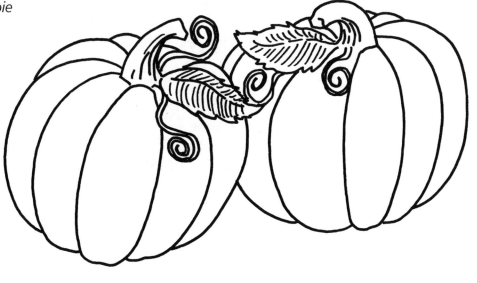

Ingredients

1 package instant vanilla pudding

½ cup milk

1 cup canned pumpkin

1½ teaspoons pumpkin pie spice

2 cups whipped topping, chilled

1 prebaked pie shell or graham cracker pie crust

Utensils

Mixing bowl

Measuring cup

Measuring spoons

Wire whisk

Large spoon

Mix the instant pudding and milk in a bowl with the wire whisk. Whip it until it's completely mixed. It will begin to thicken. Stir in the canned pumpkin and pumpkin pie spice, then gently stir in the whipped topping.

Spoon the mixture into the pie crust. Refrigerate several hours until firm.

PIES WERE A popular colonial food. Meat pies, usually made from bear meat, were an early favorite. The cook would add dried fruits, nuts, and spices to the chopped meat. *Mince meat* pies are still enjoyed today—but without the bear meat! Today's mince pie is made of spicy chopped fruit.

HERE'S A LETTER one girl wrote to a friend back in England:

Mistress Bradford invented the plan of mixing the baked pompion pulp with the meat of the Indian corn, and made of the whole a queer looking bread, which some like exceedingly well, but Father says he is forced to shut his eyes while eating it.

Spanish Rice

Spanish colonies were settled in Florida, South Carolina, and Louisiana. Also, Spanish colonies were settled in the west, along the California coastline, and inland in what is now New Mexico. Spanish exploration parties traveled into Kansas and Colorado, too.

Here's a dish that the Spanish colonists brought with them. Back in Spain it was called *paella* (say it: pie-ay-yuh).

4 servings

Ingredients

- 1 box flavored rice mix (like Rice-a-Roni)
- 1 6-ounce can black pitted olives, chopped
- 1 medium tomato, washed and chopped
- 1 4-ounce can Vienna sausages or other small, cooked sausages, chopped

Utensils

Frying pan with lid

Wooden spoon

Fork

Plate

THE FIRST SPANISH settlements were a fort at St. Augustine (now in Florida) and a mission in the Chesapeake Bay area. The mission didn't last long, but what a surprise the first English colonists at Jamestown had in 1607—the Native North Americans they met spoke *Spanish*!

(Adult help suggested.) Prepare the rice dinner following the directions on the box. For the last 15 minutes of cooking time, add the tomato, olives, and sausages. Cover and continue cooking. Serve on a plate and share it with friends.

NATIVE AMERICANS LIVING in what is now Mexico planted corn, squash, pumpkins, tomatoes, peppers, sweet potatoes, and avocados. They also enjoyed chocolate and vanilla. All of these were new foods to the Spanish colonists. The Spanish brought new foods to the Native Americans, too. Milk, cheese, raisins, beef, and wheat flour were unknown previously in the New World.

New World Cocoa Mix

S panish explorers found the Native North Americans in the New World drinking a syrupy beverage called *chocolatl*. The Spaniards tried the drink, adding sugar, and sometimes vanilla and cinnamon. They liked it and it was soon very popular in Europe.

Ingredients

1 8-quart box nonfat dry milk

1¾ cup (6-ounce jar) powdered nondairy coffee creamer

3½ cups (1-pound can) instant chocolate flavored drink powder (like Quik)

3 cups powdered sugar

Utensils

Large mixing bowl

Spoon

Large plastic storage container with lid

Mug

Combine and mix all the ingredients together in a large bowl. Store the mix in a tightly covered container until ready to drink. To make up a single serving, measure ¼ cup of the mix into a mug. Fill with hot water. Stir until blended.

You can make up packets of the drink mix to take on a trip or hike. Measure ¼ cup of the mix into a self-locking plastic sandwich bag for each serving. Make up a bunch of packets for everyone to enjoy!

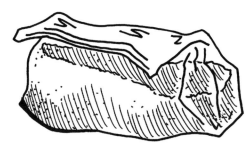

CHOCOLATE COMES FROM the seeds of a bean that grows on cacao trees. The seeds are fermented, roasted, shelled, and ground up to make chocolate. Cacao trees only grow in warm climates.

Everyday Life

Everybody worked hard in the colonies. There was wood to gather and chop, animals to care for, gardens to weed and water, and tools and household goods to make. Neighbors often relied on each other for help, often trading or lending each other any extra supplies.

Most days were spent working hard. After dark, more chores needed to be done such as wood carving or mending. These were done by candlelight that came from homemade candles. Frugal families tried to get by with using only two or three candles per night. You could call these *close-knit families* because they had to work close together.

IN AUTUMN, PEOPLE went *nutting*. They went to the forest to gather wild nuts that had been knocked to the ground by wind and rain. Sometimes they called these excursions *nutting parties*.

Homemade Cough Syrup

People had to make most of their own medicines, too. Here are two interesting ways to cure a cough. Which one would you choose?

Here's a recipe to cure a cough from a 1694 *receipt* book (what we call a recipe book):

Take 30 garden snails & 30 Earth worms of middling sise, bruise ye snails & wash them and ye worms in fair water, cut ye worms in pieces. Boil these in a quart of Spring water to a pint. Pour it boiling hot on 2 ounces of Candied Eringo root sliced thin. When it is cold strain it thro' a flannel bag. Take a quarter of a pint of it warm, with an Equal quantity of Cow's Milk. Continue this course till well.

The Receipt Book of Mrs. Ann Blencowe, 1694

Here's another homemade cough syrup recipe:

Take a half pound of the best honey and squeeze the juice of four lemons upon it; mix them well together, and add a small portion of sugar candy. A teaspoonful may be taken every time the cough is troublesome, and in a short time, a cure will be effected.

Housekeeper's Book, 1838

Here's a cough syrup recipe you can make that will work *and* taste good.

Ingredients

2 tablespoons of honey

¼ teaspoon lemon juice

Utensils

Small cup

Small jar with tight-fitting lid, like a baby food jar

1 tablespoon-size spoon

Stir the honey and lemon juice together, mixing thoroughly. Store it in a covered jar if you don't use it right away. Take 1 tablespoon full or a little more until the tickle goes away. Take as needed.

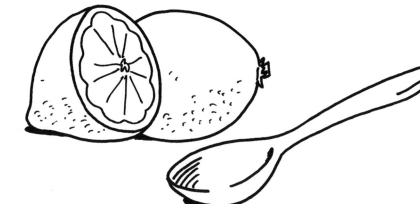

TO STOP A baby's teething pain, mothers were advised to scratch the baby's gums with an osprey bone or hang teeth from a fawn or wolf fangs around the baby's neck.

Dipped Candles

Colonists had to make their own candles. In Europe, candles were made by melting animal fat to make tallow. But cows and pigs were too precious to butcher, so they had no tallow. What could they use?

Native North Americans showed colonists how to make candles by cooking berries—little red and white berries from the bayberry bush—to make candle wax.

But a candle had to have a wick, too, and string was precious. So they gathered and stripped milkweed plants to get a fine white thread that could be used for candle wicks.

To dip candles, a willow stick was tied with several pieces of wick made from the milkweed plant. The wicks were dipped a number of times into a tub of hot wax, each time allowing the wax to dry and harden. This way, thick candles could be made that would burn a long time. Tinsmiths made metal candle molds that could be used, too.

You can make some candles, too, but you'll need a grown-up's help. Hot wax can be dangerous because it can burn your skin or burst into flame if it gets too hot.

8 pairs of 4-inch candles

ANOTHER METHOD OF making candles used beeswax. Colonists searched the forests for bee hives, ate the sweet honey, and saved the wax for candles.

Materials

Newspaper

2 large soup or juice cans, empty and opened at 1 end

Water

Measuring cup

Saucepan

1 pound of candle wax (available in craft supply stores) or old candles (check a thrift store or ask friends to save them for you)

1 package of candle wicks (available in craft supply stores)

Saucepan

1 wire hanger

Scissors

Optional

Crayons (to color wax)

Candle coloring oils

Scented oils

(Adult help strongly suggested.)

Cover the work area with newspaper.

Fill ⅓ of 1 can with water and put this can in the saucepan. Fill the saucepan half full with hot water and place it on the stove over low heat.

Fill ⅔ of the other can with cool water and set it aside on the newspapers.

Break the wax into chunks and put it into the can of hot water in the pan. (It may seem strange to mix wax with water, but they won't really mix. The wax will float to the top of the water. The water makes it easier to dip candles and uses a lot less wax.)

When the wax has melted, turn the stove off.

Cut a piece of wick about 10 inches long. Fold the wick in the center and dip both ends into the melted wax. The hot wax will stick to the wick as you pull it back up, making two candles at once.

As soon as you've pulled the wick out of the hot wax, dip it

Dip in melted wax and then cold water. Repeat.

into the can of cold water to cool it. Repeat the dipping and cooling step. After two or three dips, straighten the wick by pulling it gently so your candles will be straight.

Stop dipping when the candles are the size you want. Let the candles cool completely before storing by hanging them over the bottom of a wire hanger. When you are ready to use them, cut the wick in the center.

You can make colorful candles by dropping pieces of crayon into the hot wax, letting them melt, then stirring to mix the color through. Also, you can buy special candle coloring and/or scented oils to make your candles even more special.

Why not count how many candles you'll need in your family for the coming year's birthdays, and make them all at once? Remember, candles for birthday cakes don't have to be too big or thick.

Floating Lamps

Little lamps were made by pouring fat into metal shells and sticking wicks in them before the wax hardened. Colonists called these *Betty lamps*.

Make some little candles to float in a bowl of water.

Fill the shells with wax. Add a wick before the wax hardens.

Float them in a bowl of water for a brilliant party decoration.

Materials

Newspaper

6 or 8 clam shells or halves of walnut shells

¼ pound candle wax (available in craft supply stores)

1 large soup or juice can, empty and opened at 1 end

Double boiler

Pot holder or oven mitt

Candle wick cut into 6 or 8 2-inch pieces (available at craft supply stores)

Scissors

(Adult help strongly recommended.)

Spread out newspaper to cover the work area.

Place several shells, face up, on the newspaper. Place the wax in an empty soup can over a double boiler. Have an adult help melt and pour the wax into each shell. Fill the shell to the rim with warm wax. Before the wax hardens, place 1 2-inch wick in each shell.

To burn these little candles, fill a pretty bowl with water, place the candles on top and light. They make a nice birthday or holiday centerpiece at the dinner table.

ENGLISH COLONISTS DRANK from cups made of leather coated with wax. French colonists teased them saying the English, "drank out of their boots."

Weave a Square

Colonists made cloth from wool sheared from their sheep or from the linen fibers of flax plants.

Sometimes neighbors would weave for each other taking, in return, extra corn and apples as payment. As towns grew, weavers set up shops. People took their wool to them to be woven into cloth. Traveling weavers stayed with a family while they did the weaving.

Colonial looms were big and made from wood. Here's how to make a little one from cardboard. You can make a potholder or hot pad on it.

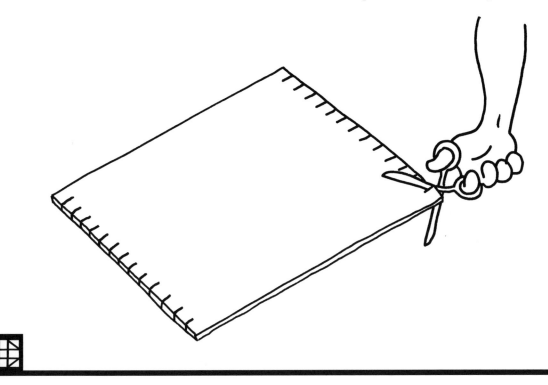

Materials

1 12 by 12-inch piece of cardboard (use the thick kind, from grocery boxes)

Pencil

Ruler

Scissors

10 yards of yarn (rolled in a ball, it's easier to work with)

Measure and mark slits along two opposite edges of the cardboard. Make the slits about ½-inch deep and ½-inch apart. Use the ruler to keep them even. Count the slits on each side and make certain you end up with an uneven number of slits. (This uneven number will make an even number of tabs.) Cut the slits with scissors.

Thread the *warp* by pushing the end of the yarn firmly into the first top left slit. (Weavers use the term warp to refer to the yarn that runs up and down on a loom.)

Bring the yarn around the tab and wind it 3 times. Pull a length of yarn to the bottom slit, going around the tab next to it and coming up at the slit. Keep doing the same thing, until the yarn has stretched back and forth behind the slits. Wind the last tab three times. Cut the yarn from the ball of yarn.

Now make the *weft*. (Weft is what weavers call the crosswise threads that are woven between the warp threads.) Cut several pieces of yarn 16-inches long. Start

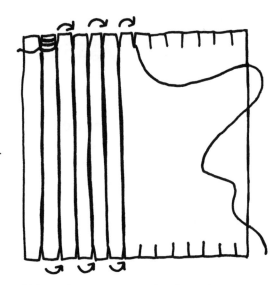

Wrap the warp yarn back and forth around the slits.

at the top of the loom and weave the yarn over the first warp, under the second, over the third, and then under. Keep making the over-under pattern.

When you get to the other end of the loom, pull the yarn so there is an even amount sticking out on both sides of the square. Start the next weft piece going under, then over. Keep adding more weft pieces, weaving them opposite to the last in the over-under pattern.

Keep going until the whole loom is covered. Then carefully tie each pair of yarn ends at the sides in knots. Bend the loom, so the weaving can be popped off the tabs. Pull the loom off the weaving.

Weave the weft yarns in and out to make a pattern.

Knit a Pouch

Stockings, sweaters, and caps weren't woven, they were *knitted* from wool thread. Girls could knit stockings by the time they were four years old. Boys knitted suspenders to hold up their trousers.

During winter months the whole family knitted socks and mittens. They sold or traded away any extras.

Children knitted pouches for soldiers to carry supplies in. Also, girls made knit pouches for their boyfriends. Make one for yourself!

Tie on a slip knot to start.

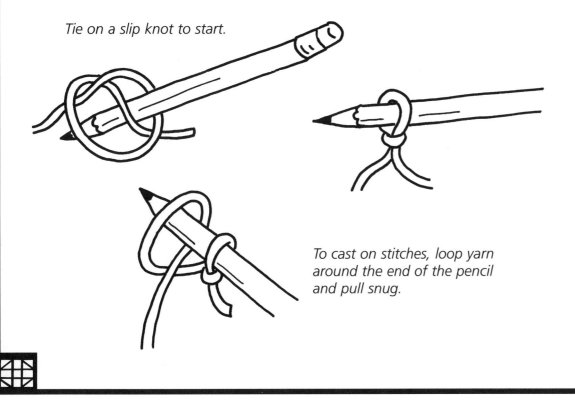

To cast on stitches, loop yarn around the end of the pencil and pull snug.

Materials
Skein of yarn
2 sharp pencils or knitting needles
Scissors
Hand sewing needle
Matching color thread

Tie a slip knot in the end of the yarn and slip the loop over a pencil point. Use it to *cast on* 15 stitches. To cast on, loop yarn around the end of the pencil as shown and pull snug. Each loop on the pencil is called a stitch.

Begin the knitting by poking the left pencil point into the stitch on the right pencil, then wrap yarn around the left pencil, and pull it through the stitch to make a new loop. It may help you to remember the steps to each stitch by repeating the following as you work: poke—wrap around—pull through—slide off. Keep knitting row after row until the piece is at least 8-inches long.

Bind off at the end and knot the last stitch. To bind off, work 2 loose stitches. With the left pencil, lift the first stitch *over* the second stitch and off the right pencil. This is one stitch bound off. Keep going until all the stitches are bound off. Knot the end of the yarn so your piece won't unravel.

Thread the needle with a doubled length of thread and knot the ends. Fold the knitted piece, inside out, with the edges together. Stitch down both sides, and knot the thread to secure.

To make a handle, cut 3 pieces of yarn, each 18-inches long. Knot the 3 together at one end. Slide the knot in a dresser drawer to hold it. Braid the 3 yarns by following this pattern: left side over, right side over left, and so on. Continue until you come to the end of the 3 pieces of yarn. Knot securely. Use the needle and thread to stitch both ends of the handle to the little purse.

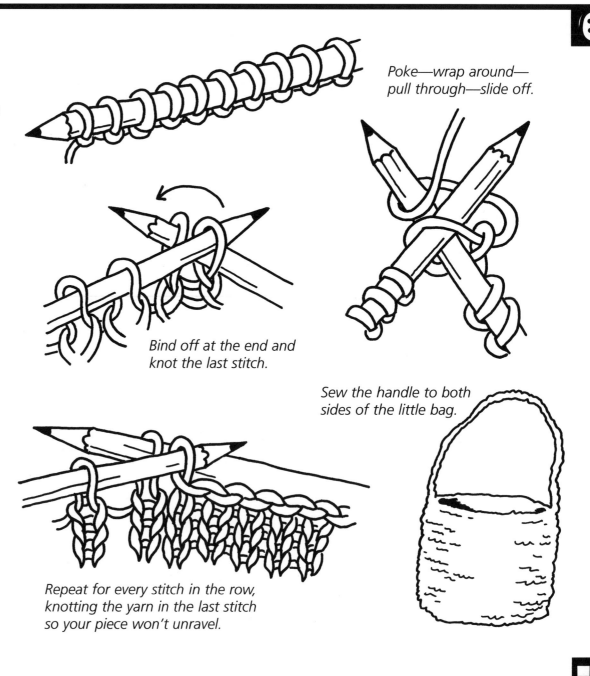

Poke—wrap around— pull through—slide off.

Bind off at the end and knot the last stitch.

Sew the handle to both sides of the little bag.

Repeat for every stitch in the row, knotting the yarn in the last stitch so your piece won't unravel.

Piece a Quilt

Since fabric had to be woven by hand, every scrap was precious. People held quilting parties so they could exchange scraps and fabric pieces to get different colors. Colonists made the pieces into a *patchwork*, laying the pieces in pretty designs before stitching the whole thing together.

Glue lace trim around the quilt block.

Materials

Pencil

Scrap paper

Ruler

1 9 by 12-inch piece of felt

Fabric scraps

Ruler

Iron-on adhesive bonding fabric

Fabric glue

1¼ yards ruffled lace trim

Practice making a few designs on scrap paper first. When you find one you like, use the ruler and pencil to draw the shapes to fit onto the felt square. Follow directions on the adhesive bonding fabric or use fabric glue to stick the fabric scraps in place on the felt.

Apply fabric glue to the edge of the gathered lace trim and press it in place around the border of the felt piece to cover the raw edges.

LOG CABIN QUILT

CRAZY QUILT

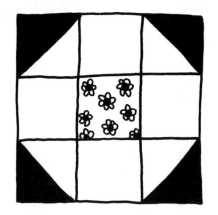

SHOO FLY

Make Soap

Colonists took a bath once a week, usually on Saturday, so they were fresh and clean for church on Sunday. A bath was no easy matter. Buckets of water had to be carried in from the well, heated over the fireplace in kettles and poured into a big tub set up in front of the fireplace. In winter, no one took baths—it was too cold in the house.

Like most everything else, colonists had to make their own soap. It was a hard job, using barrels of wood ashes and animal fat. Ashes from the fireplace were saved in a barrel with holes in the bottom. Boiling water was poured over the ashes. The tea-colored liquid that drained from the barrel was called *lye*. This was collected and saved. It took weeks to drain several barrels of ashes to get enough lye to make soap. The lye was cooked with animal fat that had been trimmed from meat. The mixture hardened when it cooled and could be cut in chunks to make bars of soap.

Soap making was a lot of work, and it all had to be done outdoors. If a family didn't make enough soap for the whole winter, they went without. (Phew!)

Here's a fun soap project that's not so much work.

Materials
Old bits and pieces of bar soap
Water
Container with a lid
Oil fragrance (optional)
Empty soft soap container

You can be as frugal as a colonist and make something useful from something that otherwise would be tossed out.

Put some bits of bar soap in a container. Cover the soap with water. Add more bits of soap and keep the water over the top of the soap so it will all dissolve. When you have at least a cup of soapy mixture, with all the soap dissolved, stir to mix it well. Add a few drops of essential oil fragrance if you like.

Refill an empty soft soap container with your recycled soap mixture.

LAUNDRY WASN'T DONE in winter. Blankets and sheets would never dry in the cold houses. Families had a lot of towels, sheets, and blankets so they could wait to do spring laundry. A proper household owned more than twenty bedsheets, which they called _rugs_.

Target Practice

Most colonists had never hunted before coming to the New World because the forests and wild animals belonged to the King or nobles. Hunting the King's deer was considered *poaching* (stealing) and punished severely—sometimes with death.

When colonial hunters saw how hard it was to hunt deer and bear, they practiced their aim. *Shot* (round lead balls) and bullets were expensive, so they were careful not to waste them when they went hunting. After shooting at targets, they used pocket knives to dig the lead bullets out of the tree so they could be remelted and reused. Also, people would go back to the site of a battle, gather up the lead, and remelt it.

Here's one way to practice your own aim.

Materials

6 empty plastic soda bottles, all the same size

Small ball or roll up a sock and wind a rubber band over it to hold its shape

Crayon or marker

Write a number on the side of each bottle. Set them apart from each other at least 10 feet from where you will stand.

HOW DID COLONISTS travel? Whenever possible, they traveled by boat on streams and rivers. The earliest roads for travel followed the Native North American trails. These were only two- or three-feet wide!

Few people traveled on horseback because horses were too valuable. They were needed to pull plows and farm wagons.

Carriages were useless because someone had to go ahead and chop fallen trees and clear the road. The axle had to be kept greased all the time, too. It was too much bother. People walked everywhere. Rich people could pay to be carried in a sedan chair, held up by two to four carriers who walked.

Take aim with the ball and make one throw at each bottle. Add up the numbers on the bottles you toppled over to get your score. Set up the bottles again and challenge yourself. Do you improve with practice? If you are playing with other children, keep score—the first person to 50 points, wins.

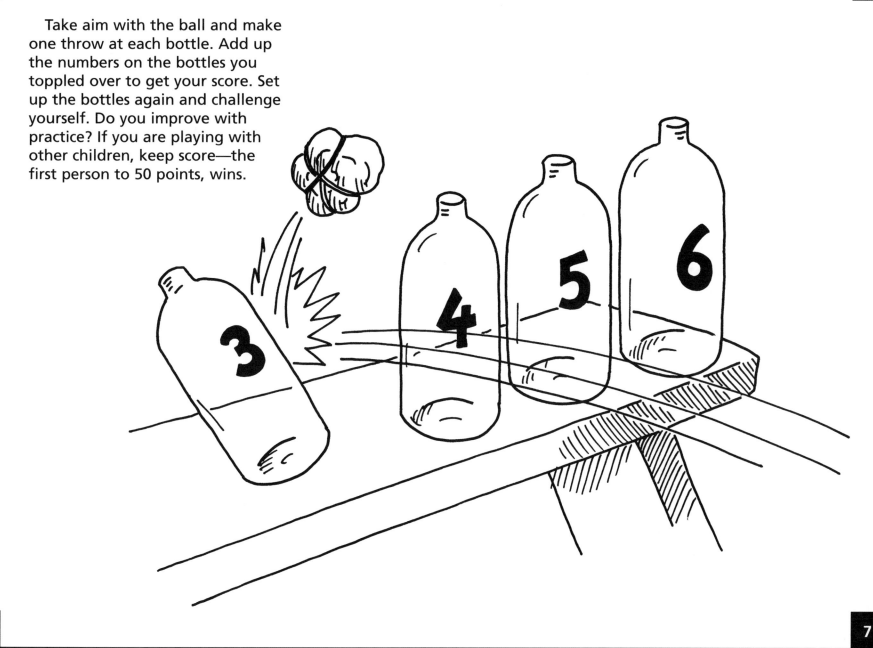

Plant a Garden

Materials

Corn seeds

Bean seeds

Utensils

Shovel

Rake

Watering can

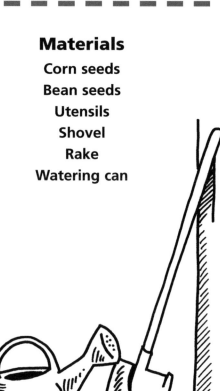

Y̲ou might think that the first colonists planted gardens right away, especially since they were running out of food. But they didn't! Most spent their time looking for gold or arguing over who would be in charge of the settlement.

It took good leaders like John Smith, for example, to force the people to work. He (and others) made laws that if a colonist didn't work, he didn't eat. People were punished with whip lashings to make them do their share of the work. Many colonial settlements failed because the people wouldn't do any work.

Many of the colonists had never lived on a farm before. The Native North Americans taught many colonists how to plant gardens. They taught the colonists to plant four corn seeds in each hole: one for each direction—north, south, east, and west. They put a piece of dead fish (herring or shad) into the hole for fertilizer. The decaying fish provided nutrients that made the plant grow better. (Today's gardeners still use fish fertilizer. It's sold in bottles to put on plants.)

Indian gardens included corn, bean, pumpkins, squash, and gourds. All are fun plants to garden with because they grow quickly and spread out to cover a lot of ground.

It's easy to grow a garden and a lot of fun, too. Here's how to grow one that's *Indian-style*.

Find a sunny spot outdoors when the soil is dry and flaky in late spring or early summer. Till the soil by lifting and turning it with a shovel. Break up clods with a rake. Pick out any rocks and sticks. Rake the ground smooth, then rake the dirt into little hills, about 1-foot across and 4-inches high.

In each hill, plant 4 corn seeds in the center, about 1-inch apart. Around the edge of the hill, plant 6 to 8 pole bean seeds. Keep the soil moist as the plants sprout and grow.

The corn will grow up tall in the center, and the bean plants will grow upon the corn for support.

Mind Your Manners!

People in colonial times behaved much like today—it was rude to interrupt when someone was speaking, people said "please" and "thank you," and it was important to behave properly so that others would want you around. But some colonial manners are very different from the good manners we practice today.

People tossed their garbage into the streets. At night, pigs were let loose to eat it all. You would certainly watch where you stepped when you were going somewhere!

People didn't brush their teeth as much as today. The toothbrushes they did use were made by fraying the end of a twig. There was no toothpaste. They used salt, sand, even ground-up bricks to clean their teeth. *Tooth rakes* were advertised for sale in newspapers.

FALSE TEETH WERE sold to wear for display or talking, but they couldn't be worn while eating. They were made of wood or gold.

Dentists advertised to buy "live teeth" that they would insert into the gums of customers. These healthy teeth were pulled out of one person's mouth and planted in someone else's mouth. Imagine needing money that badly!

Most colonists were toothless by the age of twenty. They blamed it on tea drinking and eating warm bread.

When it was mealtime, adults used chairs to sit at the table. The children were expected to stand while they ate. Eventually each family had enough furniture so everyone could be seated.

Children didn't speak to adults (even their parents) without being spoken to first. Speaking out of turn could be punished with the *rod* (a stick).

People draped big cloth napkins over one shoulder to wipe their hands on while they ate. They didn't use forks, but used their fingers to feed themselves most of the time. Forks were only used to hold meat on the trencher for cutting. It was considered bad manners to put food into your mouth with a fork.

Quaker colonists used the words *thee* and *thou* when speaking to someone. They felt the word *you* was confusing, because it didn't tell how many people were being spoken to. They used *thee* when talking to one person, and *thou* when talking with more than one person. Try it in a conversation.

Here are some "Rules of Civility and Decent

Behavior in Company," that a thirteen-year-old boy wrote down. The boy was George Washington, the same George Washington who later became the first president of the United States. Maybe his good manners helped him succeed.

Every action in company ought to be a sign of respect to those present.

In the presence of others, sing not to yourself, nor drum with your fingers or feet.

Speak not when others speak, and sit not when others stand.

Let your countenance be pleasant, but in serious matters, somewhat grave.

Show not yourself glad at the misfortunes of others.

When a man does all he can, though it succeeds not well, blame not him who did it.

Let your recreations be manful, not sinful.

Use no reproachful language against anyone, neither curses or reviling.

Gaze not at the blemishes of others, and ask not how they came.

Be not angry at the table, especially if there are strangers, for good humor makes one dish a feast.
Manners and Morals of Long Ago, 1993

He was pretty smart, wasn't he? Wouldn't it be great if everyone you met followed those rules today?

IN COLONIAL DAYS and on into the 1800s, hosts always escorted their guests part of the way home. The host walked with them to a turning point in the road, to a stream, or to a bend in the trail. It showed you cared about the visitors and was a mark of good manners.

Muster Day

There was nearly always a threat of war during the early colonial years. Colonies had their own *militias* to protect people from attacks by Native North Americans or by soldiers from other countries trying to take over the colony.

All of the colony's men and boys belonged to the militia—failure to do so put everyone in danger, so lazy men were punished. Since every village had to defend itself against intruders, everyone had to practice target shooting and marching. Throughout the year, special days were set aside to train the troops. These became holidays known as *Muster Day*. On Muster Day, which was held at different times throughout the year, men and boys practiced their marksmanship and competed for prizes. People competed in foot races, games, and other contests. Booths were set up and special treats were sold, like gingerbread, peanuts, sweet cakes, and pumpkin bread.

People set up tents to dine under while they watched the men march to the rhythm of the trumpets and drums.

Practice marching with some friends. If there are several people, make up a drill. It helps to have someone counting out the beats with a drum made from a pan and spoon. At first it might be hard to get everyone in step, but practice makes it easier—just like in the colonies.

DURING THE ENGLISH wars in Scotland, many Scots became prisoners of war. Oftentimes, they were shipped to the colonies and sold. The Massachusetts Militia wouldn't allow Scots (or Native North Americans or blacks) to join—all were considered potential enemies of the English.

Soldiers' Hardtack

During the Revolutionary War, children made cartridges, ran bullets to the soldiers, made wallets (soldiers' bags), and baked biscuits (soldiers' food).

Here's how to make the hardtack biscuit that soldiers ate.

2 dozen 2-inch-round biscuits

Ingredients

3 cups flour

1 cup plus 1 tablespoon water

Utensils

Mixing bowl

Measuring cup

Measuring spoons

Rolling pin

Biscuit cutter or drinking glass

Baking sheet, greased with shortening

Fork

Hot broth or warm cocoa

Preheat oven to 450° F. Add water to the flour and mix thoroughly to make a soft (but not sticky) dough. Dust flour on the tabletop to keep the dough from sticking. Knead and punch the dough on the tabletop for about 10 minutes. The dough will become elastic, like chewing gum.

Roll the dough out ½-inch thick and cut in circles with a biscuit cutter or the rim of a drinking glass.

Lay the biscuits on the baking sheet. Prick them a couple of times with a fork to keep air bubbles from forming as they bake.

Bake for 7 minutes. Turn the oven down to 350° F and bake 7 to 10 minutes more. The biscuits should be hard as a rock.

Hardtack never spoiled. Soldiers sometimes ate it years after it was baked.

To help soften these up, try soaking them in a cup of hot broth or warm cocoa.

Make a Diary

Children practiced perfect handwriting in a copy book they made by sewing pieces of paper together.

As soon as they were old enough to write, children kept diaries; adults did, too. Writing down the weather, what work they had done, and how much they had spent, helped them keep track of what was happening in their lives. Most colonial diaries only tell what happened, they don't tell us what the writer was feeling.

Why not make a special diary for yourself, so you can write about your own life?

Materials

Composition or spiral notebook

Polyester fleece (available in fabric shops), large enough to cover the notebook when opened up

Pencil

Scissors

½ yard of ½-inch wide ribbon

2 fabric pieces, each large enough to cover the notebook when opened up plus 2 inches all around

Craft glue

(Adult help suggested.)
Open the notebook and lay the cover on the fleece. Trace around the edge of the notebook, and cut along the tracing.

Open the notebook and lay the cover on the fabric. Trace around the edges. Add a 2-inch border all the way around the notebook, mark it, and then cut the fabric on this line.

Lay the piece of fabric you just cut onto the other piece of fabric, trace around the rest of the fabric, and use it to trace another piece the same size. Cut this out, too.

Fold one of the fabric pieces in half. Cut along the fold.

Glue the fleece to the outside of the notebook's cover. Close the notebook so you can adjust the fleece to fit along the spine. If it's too tight, the book's cover won't close easily.

Lay the notebook on the wrong side of the fabric piece. Fold the edges of the fabric over the cover and glue to the notebook. At the spine, you can't glue the fabric, so snip the fabric to the notebook's edge in 2 places, about ½-inch apart at the spine.

If you want to add a ribbon bookmark, glue about 2 inches of the ribbon to the back inside cover, next to the spine.

Take the fabric piece you cut in half and use the 2 sections for *endpapers*. Press ½-inch under all

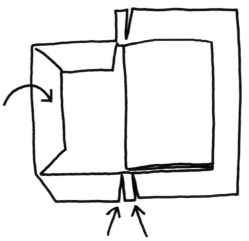

Add 2 inches all around when cutting the fabric for the cover.

around the outer edges. Spread glue along the folded under edge and press gently. This will cover the front and back inside covers as well as provide a decorative trim for the outside of the notebook.

Use a toothpick or pencil point to push the snipped ends to the inside at the spine. (Or, you can just trim them with scissors.) If there are any raw edges, dab a bit of glue to keep them from fraying.

Turn edges to the inside and glue. Snip fabric at spine.

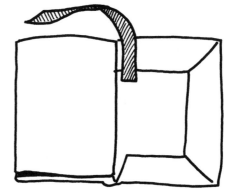

Glue ribbon in back for a bookmark.

What's Your Name?

A lot of babies died from disease in the colonies and in Europe. No one knew about germs then. Many parents feared their baby might die, so they didn't give him or her a name until it was several months old. They were just called "Baby Smith," or "Baby Jones."

Colonial babies were given their names at christening ceremonies held in churches. These were ceremonies to name babies and welcome them into the church.

In colonial times, children were sometimes given names of traits that parents thought were important. Here are the names of some children that were on the Mayflower: Remember, Resolved, Desire, and Humility. These are all first names. Other colonial children were named Patience, Charity, Unity, Experience, Waitstill, Preserved, Thanks, Unite, and Supply. (Phew!)

Many colonial babies were named after people in the bible. Some were named after their parents. Some children today are still named the same way. Ask your parents why they chose the name they gave you.

Think up some names you wish you had been given—use traits, look some names up in a bible, or in your favorite book. Maybe you'll discover you're very happy with your own name.

A FEW WEEKS after a baby's birth, the new mother gave a feast for all her women friends. Called a *groaning party*, it was a dinner of rich meats, pies, and tarts. A *groaning cake* was made when the child was born and pieces were served to visitors for several weeks. We don't know exactly why the women called it that. What do you think?

Groaning Cake

You can make a special cake to celebrate a new baby in your home, or in your friend's home. Groaning cakes are similar to what we call fruitcake today. Here's an easy recipe.

1 loaf

Ingredients

1 egg

1 cup water

1 tablespoon oil

1 package Quick Bread Mix

1 cup chopped nuts

1 cup raisins

1½ cups candied fruit

Utensils

Mixing bowl

Spoon

Bread pan, greased with shortening and dusted with flour

Knife

 (Adult help suggested.) Preheat oven to 350° F. Mix the egg, water, and oil in a bowl. Stir in the rest of the ingredients. Stir until everything is mixed together. Pour the batter into the greased and floured pan.

Bake for 1 hour and 15 minutes. Let the cake cool in the pan for 30 minutes. Loosen the edges with a knife, and remove the cake from the pan. Cut into slices to serve.

You can make this cake before the baby comes home from the hospital. When wrapped, it will keep in the refrigerator for 2 weeks; in the freezer for 3 months. Groaning Cake might be a fun new tradition to start in your family.

Make an Almanac

One of the few things colonial families bought each year was a new almanac. An *almanac* is a book full of facts and information. Settlers wanted to know the best days for planting crops and the dates of holidays. Almanacs told the position of stars and planets and predicted the weather. They had advice about farming, cooking, health, and love. Almanacs usually contained predictions about the future based on the positions of stars and planets. Today we call this *astrology*.

NEW ENGLAND COLONISTS had three big celebrations each year:

Commencement Day (School and college graduation day was a big event because these colonists valued education. Church ministers moved graduation ceremonies to Fridays to stop people from celebrating all week long.)

Muster Day

Election Day (Election Day followed a week of excitement and holiday fun. 'Lection Cake, a special fruitcake, was served.)

Enterprising colonists wrote almanacs and paid printers to print them up. Almanacs were sold in shops or by door-to-door peddlers. People who wrote almanacs tried to make theirs better than anyone else's, so they added jokes, riddles, poems, and artwork.

Benjamin Franklin wrote the most popular almanac. He called it *Poor Richard's Almanac*. (Franklin might have chosen this title because other popular almanacs contained first names in their titles and the adjective "poor" such as *Poor Robin* and *Poor John*. Franklin started using the pen name Richard Saunders when he was a printer and publisher in Philadelphia.) He sold more than 140,000 copies of it.

The Old Farmer's Almanac is still printed and sold every year. It has been sold every year for more than two hundred years!

You can make an almanac for your own use.

Materials

Notebook

Calendar

Old magazines and newspapers

Pens and pencils

Scissors

Paste or tape

Ruler

Draw 12 monthly calendar grids, 1 on every other page of the notebook, for each month of the year. (Refer to a calendar to pencil in the days and dates for each month.)

In addition to these holidays, add your family birthdays, anniversaries, special events, vacations, and the first and last days of school.

Cut out jokes, cartoons, and interesting items from newspapers and magazines. Paste them in your almanac. Write down some advice, goals, and things you don't want to forget.

Record the following holidays in your almanac:

Holiday/Event	Date
New Year's Day	January 1
Martin Luther King Day	Third Monday in January
Chinese New Year	Second new moon of winter
Groundhog Day	February 2
Valentine's Day	February 14
St. Patrick's Day	March 17
First day of Spring	March 21
Passover	Varies, ask someone
Easter	Varies, ask someone
April Fool's Day	April 1
Earth Day	April 22
Cinco de Mayo	May 5
Mother's Day	Second Sunday in May
Memorial Day	Last Monday in May
Flag Day	June 14
Father's Day	Third Sunday in June
First day of Summer	June 21
Independence Day	July 4
Labor Day	First Monday in September
First day of Autumn	September 23
Columbus Day	October 12
Halloween	October 31
Thanksgiving	Fourth Thursday in November
First day of Winter	December 21
Hanukkah	Varies, ask someone
Christmas	December 25
Kwanzaa	December 26 to January 1

Here's an old saying (from the year 1562) that helps us remember how many days are in each month:

Thirty days hath November,
April, June, and September.
February hath 28 alone,
And all the rest have 31.

CHRISTMAS WASN'T CELEBRATED by the Puritans because it was a Church of England holiday and they disagreed with the church's practices. Fines were levied and anyone doing anything on December 25 that might be interpreted as a celebration was punished. Shops had to remain open and a full day's work was expected.

THE SOUTHERN COLONIES, populated by members of the Church of England, observed Christmas and Easter just as they had done in England. They celebrated Christmas on January 5, according to the old church calendar. About 1750 the date was changed to December 25.

Proverbs

A *proverb* is a short saying that tells a basic truth or practical rule about how to act or behave. Here are some proverbs people told in colonial days. Have you heard them before? Can you figure out what they mean?

Beauty is only skin deep.

All work and no play makes Jack a dull boy.

Don't bite off more than you can chew.

All for one, one for all.

Your eyes are too big for your stomach.

Early to bed and early to rise, makes a man healthy, wealthy, and wise.

He that goes a borrowing, goes a sorrowing.

Be civil to all; sociable to many; familiar with few; friend to one, enemy to none.

It's bad manners to silence a fool, and cruelty to let him go on.

Don't look a gift horse in the mouth.

A fool and his money are soon parted.

Every cloud has a silver lining.

Whatever is worth doing at all is worth doing well.

Dictionary of Quotations, 1969

Can you think of any proverbs we use today?

Wampum

What did the colonists use for money? Mostly they traded goods and labor with each other, but they needed some form of exchange when this wouldn't work. There were quite a variety of coins brought over from Europe including coins from Spain, the Netherlands, Britain, France, and Germany. Spain even had a mint located in Mexico City where Mexican silver was made into dollars or *pieces of eight*.

So many different currencies made trading confusing, and there weren't enough coins for everyone to use. Some colonists made coins from silver and gold, but they were very expensive—in fact, they still are.(Old coins minted in the colonies bring very high prices from collectors. Find one today, and you can buy your family a very nice car or house!)

The colonists wanted to buy furs from the Native North Americans because the furs could be sold in Europe for good prices. But they had to pay them something in exchange. The colonists ended up using the same things Native North Americans used for exchange: beaver skins, tobacco, or wampum.

Wampum was a string of shell beads made from clam shells. They were tiny and hard to make. There were both purple and white wampum beads. There weren't as many purple ones, so they were more valuable. The Native North Americans wore the strings of wampum as necklaces or belts because they didn't have safes or banks to store them in.

The colonists used wampum with each other, too. It became the money of the first colonies. Dutch colonists made wampum in small factories to use in trade.

White beads symbolized health, peace, and riches; purple beads, sympathy or sorrow. The darkest purple beads were the most valuable.

Make a few strings of wampum for yourself.

Materials

1 cup rubbing alcohol (or water)
Uncooked salad macaroni
Blue and red food coloring
Yarn or string

Utensils

Measuring cup
Small bowl
Spoon
Newspapers
Hair pin or tape

Knot end of yarn over the first bead to keep the beans from falling off.

Wrap tape on end of yarn to stiffen it.

You only have to color about half the macaroni. The white wampum can be made from uncolored macaroni.

Pour about 1 cup of alcohol (or water) into a small bowl. Color the water by adding blue and red food coloring, a drop at a time, until the mixture turns purple.

Drop macaroni into the colored mixture and let it sit until it is tinted as dark a purple as you want. (If you are using water instead of alcohol, don't let it sit too long or it will get sticky and gummy.) Leave macaroni in tinted water only long enough to color it.

Spoon the tinted macaroni onto newspapers and let it dry.

Once dry, string your wampum onto the yarn or string. If you have a hard time getting the yarn to pass through the macaroni, clip the end of the yarn in a hair pin and pass it through. Or, wrap a piece of tape very tightly around the end of the yarn, making it stiff.

Smallpox Parties

Colonists held *smallpox parties*, of all things! Can you believe it?

Vaccination began in Turkey. An English woman, Mary Wortley Montagu (Lady Montagu), saw how vaccines gave people immunity from disease and wrote about it. Dr. Edward Jenner began inoculating patients against smallpox in Britain in 1796. The discovery spread to the colonies where people argued (and even rioted) over it. Many thought it was too dangerous because sometimes the inoculation caused the deadly disease.

At first it horrified the colonists to see a doctor put a needle into someone's body. But when they saw that it worked, they were eager to get shots for themselves and their children. Smallpox epidemics had raged through the New World, killing many people, and leaving terrible scars on survivors.

The smallpox vaccine caused a mild bout of the disease and made the person immune against getting so severe a case that they died. After getting a shot, they developed a fever and broke out with a few red spots, but it was nothing compared to a full-blown case of smallpox.

People began to form smallpox classes where a group would get the inoculation at one time. A whole family, their friends, and all their relatives would get the shot at one time. Everyone would come down with a mild case of the illness. These became known as *smallpox parties* and invitations were sent out ahead of time. Fancy "hospitals" started up where people could spend their smallpox party time in style and luxury. After all, a person went to a smallpox party only once in a lifetime!

Check your vaccination record. Do you need to update your own immunity? Maybe you and your family could do something special the next time someone needs a vaccination. Wouldn't your friends be amazed to get invitations to a flu shot party?

Here's a guideline for some common inoculations. Check with your doctor for more information or current recommendations.

Time	Inoculation
At birth	Hepatitis B
2 months	Hepatitis B, Polio, Diphtheria, Tetanus, Pertussis, Meningitis
4 months	Hepatitis B, Polio, Diphtheria, Tetanus, Pertussis, Meningitis
6 months	Hepatitis B, Polio, Diphtheria, Tetanus, Pertussis, Meningitis
12–15 months	Measles, Mumps, Rubella, Meningitis
15 months	Diphtheria, Tetanus, Pertussis
4–6 years	Polio, Diphtheria, Tetanus, Pertussis, Measles, Mumps, Rubella
14–16 years and every 10 years after that	Tetanus

Center for Disease Control

IN COLONIAL DAYS, anyone could call themselves a doctor or physician and practice medicine. The only way to judge a good doctor was by the survival of his or her patients. Old Joe Pye and Sabbatus were two well-known Native North American doctors who treated colonists.

When a Connecticut doctor died, his black servant named Primus took over his practice. Dr. Primus was very successful as the county's doctor for many years.

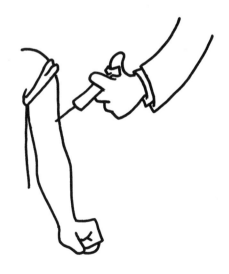

89

Lottery

otteries created the most excitement in the New England colonies. They held lotteries for everything. Almost everyone sold tickets for the drawings. Lotteries were used to help finance schools and colleges, and to build bridges and even a few libraries.

But people also held lotteries of their own, often advertising in local newspapers. They offered jewelry, books, or furniture as prizes. Many of these lotteries were frauds and rip-offs and ticket buyers lost their money.

By 1830 (long after colonial days), many people realized they were wasting their money and had little chance of winning anything. In this year, a law was passed to stop lotteries.

You can make a lottery where everyone wins!

Materials

Paper

Scissors

Pencil, pen, or marker

Large jar or can

Cut up slips of paper and write special treats on each one: stay up half an hour later than usual, get an extra dessert, choose a family television program, pick a bedtime book, choose the dinner menu, and so on. Think of as many treats as you can that you and your family will enjoy.

Fold the slips and place them in a large can, and take turns drawing chances.

A lottery can be a fun and easy way to divide up chores around the house, too.

Arts and Crafts

Even though life was hard in the colonies and people didn't have much time or money, they still made art. They used what they had or made things from very simple materials. Nothing was wasted—even things that might have been discarded were turned into works of art—like the intricate quilts made from scraps of fabric. Exercise your own creativity by making a few of the things colonists enjoyed.

Cut a Silhouette

In colonial times there were no cameras or photographs. Wealthy people hired artists to paint their portraits, but most people had a *shade* or *shadow* made of themselves. We call these *silhouettes*. Silhouettes were quick to make and didn't cost much. Hundreds of silhouette artists traveled around making people's images until the 1840s when photography became popular.

Silhouette artists used only paper and scissors. Some used a candle's light, others looked at the person's profile as they cut the paper. They tried to make it look just like the person.

Materials

Shoe box

Pencil

Scissors

Flashlight

1 2 by 3-foot piece white paper, construction paper, or butcher paper

Tape

Chair

1 piece black construction paper

Glue

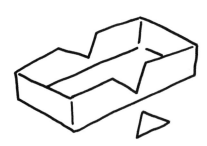

Cut Vs in the sides of the shoe box to hold the flashlight.

First, make a holder for the flashlight out of the shoe box. Cut 2 V shapes in the sides of the box so the flashlight sits across the box. Make 1 V deeper than the other, so the flashlight beam will be directed up to the wall.

Tape a large sheet of paper to the wall.

Have a friend sit in a chair in the middle of the flashlight beam. Have him or her sit so their profile shadow is cast onto the paper. You may need to adjust the paper, the person, and the flashlight to get their silhouette just right. You may need to shut off other lights close to the wall to get a dark shadow to trace.

Use a pencil to trace the edge of the shadow on the paper.

Take the paper down from the wall and cut very carefully along the line you drew.

You can either save the center cut-out silhouette and paste it to a piece of black paper, or tape a piece of black paper behind the frame of paper from which you cut the center portrait. Colonial artists did them both ways.

TWO FAMOUS AMERICAN silhouette cutters were born without hands. Martha Anne Honeywell, a young girl, cut by holding the paper with her toes and working the scissors with her mouth. A boy, Sanders Nellis, used his toes to work the scissors. Both were well-known for their good work.

Model a Figure

In colonial times it was popular to model small figures and flowers from wax. Girls took lessons on how to do *waxwork*.

Patience Wright was the first wax artist to make portraits of living people. She made life-size wax heads by looking at the person's face as she molded a chunk of wax in her lap. She tinted the faces, added wigs, made full-size bodies, and then dressed the figures in the person's own clothes. She set up the figures and charged people to look at them. She earned enough money to support her five children after her husband died.

Her collection of wax people was so popular and successful in the colonies that she was invited to make wax figures of the King and Queen of England. While she was working in London, the Revolutionary War started in the colonies. She sent messages back to the colonies about the English military plans and became our country's first woman spy.

Patience Wright started modeling small figures when she was a young child. She used soft bread for clay and made dyes to color the figures from herbs, flowers, and tree sap. You can make bread dough clay yourself.

Materials

Dry, stale white bread

Small bowl

White glue

Tablespoon

Food coloring

Toothpicks

Waxed paper

Acrylic or tempera paints or markers

Paintbrush

Tear the crusts off the bread and discard. Break the bread into small pieces. Add glue to the bread pieces, about 1 tablespoon of glue for each piece of bread. Mix with a spoon, then knead it with your fingers until it's soft and not sticky. If you want to color the clay, add drops of food coloring to a spoonful of glue and mix through. (White clay is easy to paint when dry.)

Shape small figures, using tooth-picks or your fingernails to create details. How about making rabbits, dragons, frogs, trolls, flowers, or mice? Let your imagination think of clever figures.

When finished, place the figures on wax paper and let them dry a few hours. Paint them with acrylic or tempera paints, or decorate with markers.

If you don't use all the clay, you can store it in the refrigerator in a sealed plastic bag or container.

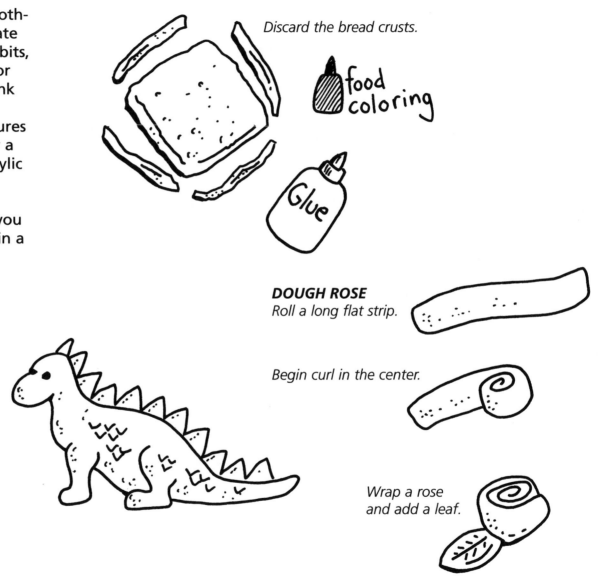

Discard the bread crusts.

food coloring

Glue

DOUGH ROSE
Roll a long flat strip.

Begin curl in the center.

Wrap a rose and add a leaf.

Decoupage: Pasted Paper

Pieces of paper were hard to come by in the colonies so every bit was saved and put to use. People made pretty items from papers they had saved.

Decoupage (say it: day-koo-paj) started in France. In French, the word means "to cut up or cut out." Decoupage is the art of cutting out pretty designs from paper and pasting them to a background. Colonists from France brought the art to North America where people pasted small cut-out pictures on boxes and vases to make them pretty.

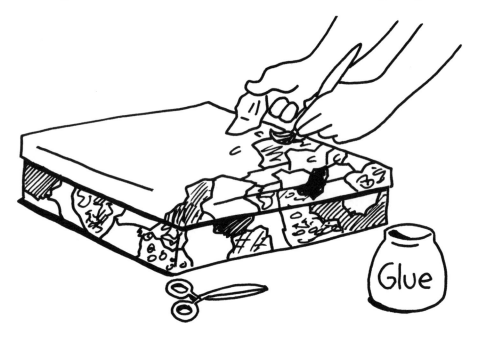

Materials

Newspapers

Magazines, catalogs, gift wrap, and/or greeting cards (to cut up)

Scissors

White glue, decoupage medium, or premixed wallpaper paste

Paint brush or foam brush

Small box with lid, to cover

Spread out the newspapers to cover the work surface.

Cut out colorful pictures that you like. Trim the edges carefully. Brush the back of each picture with glue. Press it in place on the box. Add more pictures, layering the edges over each other, until the entire box is covered.

Brush a coat of glue over the whole surface. Press down any edges that curl up. Let dry. Brush on a second coat of glue.

You can use a hair dryer to hurry the drying, so you can finish the project at one sitting.

Make a Band Box

Early Americans carried their belongings in cardboard or wooden boxes. They didn't use suitcases. The boxes were covered with wallpaper and the inside had newspapers pasted to the sides for a lining.

Band boxes were used to store white collars and ruffs, which were called *bands*. Pretty boxes were used to store wigs, caps, laces, and straw hats.

Materials
Poster board

Pencil

Scissors

Ruler

Masking tape

Glue or glue stick

Wallpaper or gift wrap

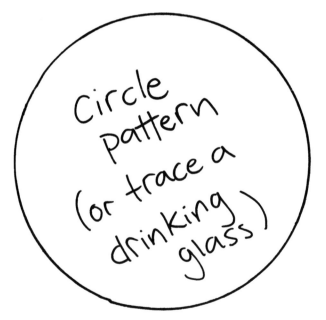

Circle Pattern (or trace a drinking glass)

POSTER BOARD:
2 CIRCLES
1 10½ BY 2-INCH STRIP
1 10½ BY 1-INCH STRIP
GIFT WRAP:
2 CIRCLES
1 10½ BY 3-INCH STRIP
1 10½ BY 2-INCH STRIP

Use the pattern here or trace around the bottom of a soup can. Trace and cut out 2 circles from the poster board.

Cut 2 strips from the poster board, 1 10½-inches long by 2-inches wide (for the side of the box) and 1 10½-inches long by 1-inch wide (for the side of lid).

Use these 4 shapes as patterns to trace and cut out the gift wrapping paper that will be used to cover the box. Cut the 2 circles just like the patterns. But, for the long strips add 1 inch to the width, so you make the strips 10½ by 3-inches and 10½ by 2-inches.

First, make the box. Tape the wider strip to form a circle. Use small strips of tape to attach it to one of the circles. Tape all the way around, overlapping the ends and taping them to lie flat.

Tape the thinner strip to form a circle. Attach it to the circle that will form the lid of the box. Center it, then tape it. Try the lid on the box to see if it fits. If it's too tight, retape, letting it out a little at the overlap on the side.

Use the pieces cut from gift wrap to cover the box. Do the sides first.

Fold the long paper strips ½ inch along one edge. Glue to board. Use scissors to snip cuts along the folded edge, about every inch. Cut to the fold, but do not paste it.

Apply a glue stick or spread glue with your fingers to the wrong side of the paper. Press the clipped edges in place along the base of

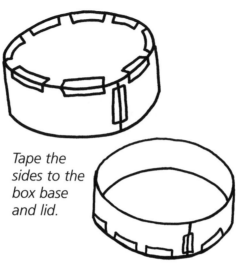

Tape the sides to the box base and lid.

the box and the lid. The snipped pieces will overlap so the paper fits around the curve. Press the paper in place on the sides and turn the edge along the rim to the inside.

Glue the circles of gift wrap to the base of the box and lid.

Use your little band box to hold candy, jewelry, coins, marbles—anything small and special.

You can make larger boxes by starting with a bigger circle. Measure the outside edge of the circle to figure out how long the side strip must be.

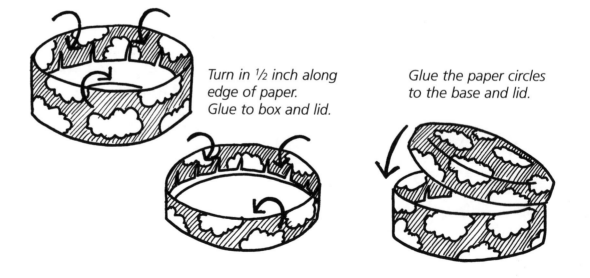

Turn in ½ inch along edge of paper. Glue to box and lid.

Glue the paper circles to the base and lid.

Paper Quilling

Quilling is the art of curling strips of paper into interesting designs. The craft got its name from the way paper strips were curled around bird quills (a feather's center backbone). Colonial artists decorated candle holders and tea trays with pretty quilling.

You only need to learn how to roll a strip of paper around a pencil—pretty easy, huh?

Glue to make a coil.

Pinch to make a teardrop shape.

Materials

White paper, foil, or gift wrap

Scissors

Pencil, round toothpick, coffee stirrer, nail, or another object to roll the strips around

White Glue

Toothpick

Egg carton

Pinch paper strip in the center, then curl ends for a heart.

Combine shapes to make clever designs.

Practice with strips of paper cut into different size widths. One-quarter-inch wide strips are a good size for many projects.

Curl the paper strip tightly around the pencil to make a coil. Use a toothpick to dot a drop of glue to hold the end of the coil in place. Then squeeze or crimp it to get the shape you want. Make up several coils, storing them by color or size in an empty egg carton.

You can use the quilled designs to decorate a greeting card, or hang them from thread to make Christmas decorations or interesting mobiles.

Pinch a Pot

Both colonists and Native North Americans used clay pots for cooking and storing food.

You can make a pinch pot to use for candy or nuts.

Use your thumb to shape the center.

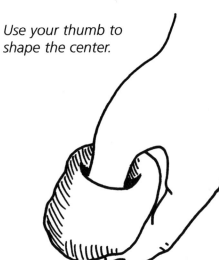

Materials

Newspapers

Red or white self-hardening clay (available in craft supply stores)

Bowl

Water

Sharp pencil, toothpick, or nail (to make designs)

Acrylic paints

Paint brush

Make designs with a toothpick.

Cover the work area with newspapers.

Roll a ball of clay about the size of a plum. Push your thumb into the center and pinch the sides up with your fingers. Add small pieces of clay to the sides to make it the size you want.

Roll a clay snake and press it in place for a handle, if you want.

Place some water in a bowl. Dip your fingertips into the water and smooth out any bumps or holes in the pot. Use a sharp object like a pencil point, toothpick, nail, or even your fingernails to make designs on the outside of the pot and along the rim. If you don't like how it looks, smooth over the designs with a dab of water and try it again.

Let it sit and dry for at least a day.

If you want to color the pot, you can use acrylic paints or give it a rubbing with a rag dipped in brown shoe polish—that will make it look antique.

Dye a Shirt or Socks

Colonists gathered plants to make dye to color their clothing. Children were usually given the job of collecting walnut shells (for brown), berries (blue or red), poplar leaves (yellow), or flowers (yellow or blue).

Use onion skins to color a white T-shirt or socks a soft shade of yellow—perfect to wear on sunny days!

Materials

Yellow-brown papery outer layers from 6 onions (Ask your grocery store manager for some when the vegetable bins are cleaned.)

Large pot

Water

Slotted spoon

Measuring spoons

Vinegar

White, all-cotton T-shirt or socks

(Adult help suggested.) Put the onion skins in the pot and cover them with water. Heat to a boil and simmer for 20 minutes. Let cool.

Scoop out the onion skins. Heat the water again and drop the T-shirt or socks into the hot dye bath.

To *set* the dye (so it won't wash out right away) add 2 tablespoons of white vinegar to the dye bath. Turn off the heat and let the shirt or socks soak in the dye for 1 hour.

Wring the clothing out and put it in a sink or pan of cool water to rinse. Wring out the clothing and let it dry.

(The color will depend on how many onion skins were used and how diluted the dye was. No 2 projects will color the same.)

Simmer the onion skins.

Drain the skins. Put the clothing in the dye bath.

Make Buttons

In Europe there were *sumptuary laws*. These laws forbade people who weren't rich or royal from wearing fancy clothing.

In the colonies, people had more freedom. Colonists could wear as many buttons, ribbons, or laces as they could afford. People made buttons from bone, sea shells, pewter, or even silver.

Materials

Oven-bake polymer clay
Toothpick
Baking sheet

(Adult help suggested.) Preheat oven to 275° F. Roll out little balls of clay all the same size. Press each ball to flatten it into a button shape. Poke two holes in the center of each with a toothpick. Place the buttons on a baking sheet and bake for about 10 minutes.

Sew your homemade buttons on your clothing or cut a heavy paper card and stitch the buttons to the paper so you can give them to someone special. Of course you can also do what the colonists did—barter with a friend and trade your buttons for something they've made.

Roll clay balls.

Flatten and poke holes in the center of each.

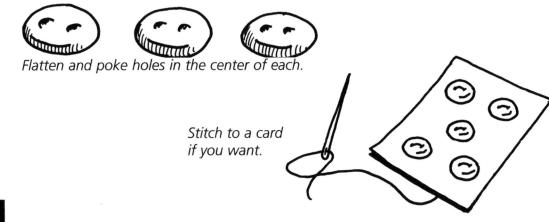

Stitch to a card
if you want.

School and Learning

Nothing was as important to colonists as education. People thought the most important thing parents could do was provide an education for their children. Every home had at least one book, the Bible, and everyone in the family learned to read and memorize passages from it. As soon as possible, children were taught to write their letters and add and subtract numbers. Schools were started right away; if there wasn't a building, they held classes in their homes. Colonists felt getting an education was important because they could read the Bible and newspapers for themselves, instead of being given the king's interpretation.

Make a Quill Pen

In school, students sat on long wooden benches. They spent the day copying the alphabet, words, and arithmetic problems onto a slate, or practicing penmanship with a quill pen. Some pen points were made of metal and screwed into wooden handles, but these pens were expensive and only used by adults. Children and people who wanted to save money used pens made from bird feathers.

Materials

1 long bird feather, a turkey feather is best (available in craft supply stores)

Knife or scissors

Bottle of ink

Paper

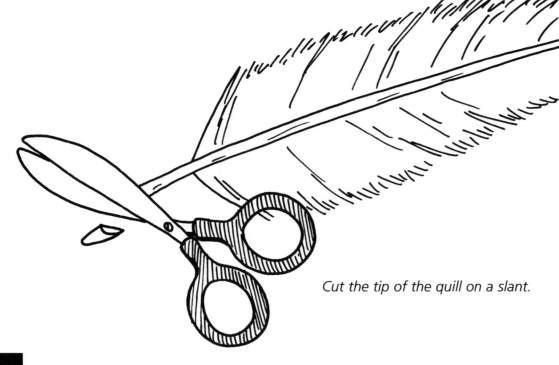

Use the knife or scissors to cut the *quill* (that's the center of the feather) at a slant. The hollow in the quill will hold ink, and the slanted point will direct the ink onto the paper. After using the pen for a while, the point will dull. You can re-cut it again just above the worn-down tip.

Cut the tip of the quill on a slant.

Homemade Ink

Once you've got the pen, you need ink. Colonists sometimes used ink powder that they mixed with water. If they didn't have powder, they had to make their own ink. Kids were responsible for bringing their own ink to school. Berry juice could be thinned with water, and worked pretty well; so did chimney soot. But most classroom inks were made at home from nut shells.

Materials

1 old sock or thick plastic zip lock bag

Hammer

12 walnut shells

Small saucepan

1 cup water

Small jar with lid

Measuring spoons

¼ teaspoon white vinegar

(Adult help suggested.) Place the shells into the sock or bag and close securely. Lightly hammer the sock to break up the shells. The more broken up the shells are, the better. Put the shells in a small saucepan and add the water. Simmer on low heat for 30 minutes. Turn the heat off and let the shells soak in the water overnight. (Quite a bit of it will have cooked away.)

Pour the brown ink you've made into a small jar and add ¼ teaspoon of white vinegar. The vinegar will keep the color from fading and the ink from spoiling.

Make a Hornbook

What a strange thing a hornbook is to us today! In colonial times, there were thousands of hornbooks sold and every child had one.

A *hornbook* wasn't a book at all. It was a wooden paddle with a thin piece of animal horn fastened to it. The horn was cut thin and soaked to shape it. It became like a piece of clear plastic. It was see-through and protected the lesson from soil. Under the piece of horn was a piece of paper that had the student's lesson on it. A lesson might be the alphabet, the Lord's Prayer, Bible verses, or arithmetic facts.

A student would wear the hornbook around his neck, hanging it from a cord, and use this as a study table since all students sat on long wooden benches without tables or desks.

SOME TEACHERS WERE known to use a student's hornbook to thump them on the head for not paying attention. Hornbooks were sold by the thousands, for ½ penny apiece.

BOYS WENT TO school, but girls didn't. Since women couldn't vote or own property, most girls weren't sent to school. They were taught at home. Girls were taught to read the Bible and newspaper. However, many girls were not taught to write.
Wealthy families hired tutors to come to their home and teach their children.

Materials

Heavy cardboard

Scissors

1 sheet clear acetate (save a piece from a shirt or stationary box)

Paper

Pen

4 paper clips

Cut the cardboard in the shape of a paddle. Cut the acetate to fit over it. Write a lesson on plain paper with a dark pen. You might want to try memorizing poetry, Bible verses, or the "Pledge of Allegiance," or a song. Slide the lesson under the acetate and clip both to the paddle using the 4 paper clips.

Once you've memorized your lesson, write a different one. Memorizing is good exercise for your mind!

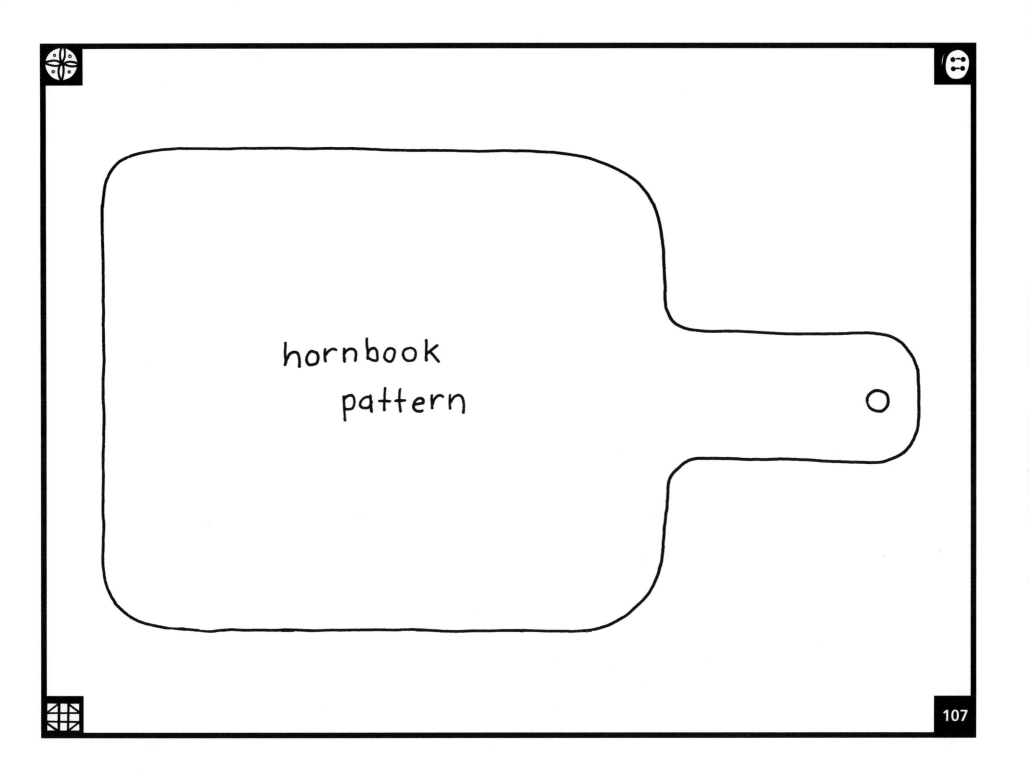

hornbook
pattern

Make a Chalk Slate

This project takes more time, but lasts longer than a cardboard hornbook. Children brought homemade wooden slates to school or used square slabs of slate rock to write on with chalk. Slate rock was cut thin and used as roof shingles, but it made a great writing surface, too. Boys were kept after school to clean the teacher's blackboard long ago.

Sand the edges of the board.

Paint the board with blackboard paint.

Write with chalk. Wipe with a rag.

Materials

1 ¼-inch piece Masonite or similar board (The lumberyard will cut it to the size you want. You can make one small enough to use on your lap or buy a big piece and make a chalkboard that fastens to your wall.)

Sandpaper

Blackboard paint (It's a special kind of paint available in paint stores.)

Paint Brush

Chalk

Rag

Use sandpaper to sand the edges of the board smooth. Follow the paint manufacturer's directions to paint the smooth side of the board. When it's dry, use blackboard chalk to write on it. Wipe it clean with a rag. When it needs to be cleaned, the rag can be dampened with water.

Stitch a Sampler

Colonial girls spent their time learning stitchery. Sewing was *very* important, as all clothing had to be made by hand. What family would want to wear clothes that were stitched together with sloppy stitches? Their clothing would fall apart. The sewing machine wasn't invented until 1830 so sewing by hand was the only option. Stitching a sampler was a way for girls to practice making neat stitches, learn the alphabet, and make something pretty to hang on the wall. Many old samplers are in museums now, and are very beautifully done—the girls were artists with thread.

Materials

Pencil

Paper

1 12-inch square of gingham-checked fabric with ⅛- or ¼-inch checks

Embroidery hoop

Embroidery needle

3 skeins of embroidery thread

Scissors

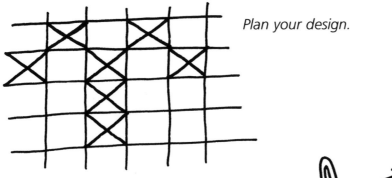

Plan your design.

This little sampler hangs on the wall inside the embroidery hoop, which becomes the frame. Practice your design on paper first, drawing little X's with a pen-

To thread the needle, crease the thread on the needle and then slip the needle's eye over the crease.

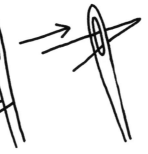

A METAL NEEDLE cost about an hour's pay for a laborer in the colonies. That would be equivalent to about five dollars or more today. Women kept their needles in cases so they wouldn't get lost or rust away.

cil. You'll use the checks of fabric to help you line up the X's as you stitch them. This will keep them in straight lines, all the same size.

Place the fabric between the 2 parts of the embroidery hoop. Make sure the center of the fabric is in the center of the hoop. Pull the fabric tight so there are no wrinkles in it.

Thread the needle. It's easy to thread thick threads if you first pinch the thread tightly around the needle, leaving an end an inch or so long. Then slide the yarn off the needle without losing the crease. Push the eye of the needle onto this loop and pull the loop through. Go ahead and thread the needle with an arm's length of thread, cut, and knot the end.

Stitch the design, following the number of X's you've planned. Change your plan if it suits you, as you go along.

Hold the hoop with one hand and pass the needle from the back to the front. Bring the needle out right next to the last stitch. As you stitch, be sure you don't pull the

stitches too tight or the fabric will pucker.

Keep stitching until you're satisfied with the results. You can add a border of X's around the center design if you like.

When finished with your design, pull the needle and thread through the back and make a stitch through each fabric corner to gather and hide the extra material behind the loop. Pull tight and knot and clip the thread. Stitch on a loop of thread or piece of ribbon so the sampler can be hung on the wall.

Pull fabric to the back and stitch to hold.

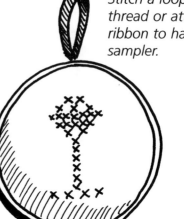

Stitch a loop of thread or attach a ribbon to hang your sampler.

Make a Bookplate

Books were important and scarce. Children were given hornbooks because they were thought to be too careless to handle real books. People lent and borrowed books from each other because there were practically no libraries. People affixed *bookplates* inside their books to show ownership or to remind lenders to return their books. Common messages included:

Steal not this book my honest friend,
For fear the gallows will be your end.

If you dare to steal this book
The devil will catch you on his hook.

This book is one thing, my fist's another,
If you touch the one, you'll feel the other.

Bookplates were used by Virginians, New Yorkers, and Pennsylvania Quakers—colonists who were a bit richer than the others. They had their own libraries and book collections. Many bookplates include the words *ex libris*. That's Latin and means "from the books." Most colonial boys were expected to learn Latin in school.

Make up a set of bookplates to write your own name on or make decorative bookplates to give as gifts.

Materials

Typing paper

Pen

Markers

Ruler

Scissors

Glue stick

Fold a piece of typing paper in half, then in half, then in half again. Unfold to get 8 rectangles. Draw over the folds with a pen. Inside each rectangle, write your bookplate message. Usually these read: *From the library of* _____ and is left blank for a name. You can leave yours blank and fill them in later or print your name carefully on each. Draw interesting borders and add decorations if you like. Make them as clever as you can.

If you want to make a lot of bookplates for your own personal library, go to a print shop and have them make several copies of your 8-bookplate sheet before cutting it. Cut them apart and paste each one in the front of a special book. That way, once you lend them to a friend, they know who to return it to.

Paste bookplates inside your books.

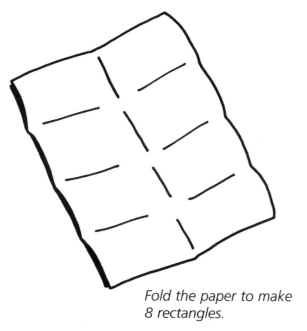

Fold the paper to make 8 rectangles.

Draw a bookplate in each space. Make copies.

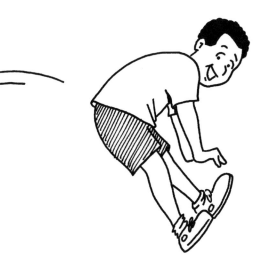

Fun and Games

olonial kids didn't spend a lot of time at play. They worked along with the grown-ups and had to go to school or study their lessons when they weren't working. But they did have fun whenever they got a chance.

Colonial kids' games were usually simple ones that didn't need special equipment. These games could be played without much set up or fuss and were played by children of all ages.

Hoop Roll

A metal hoop from a barrel was rolled along the ground using a stick to control its direction. You can try it with a large plastic hoop and a wooden spoon or ruler. Children would race each other, careful not to lose control of the hoop, over rough ground.

Honey Pot

One child is *It*. They roll up tight, knees to their chest, to become the "honey pot." The rest of the players try to lift up the honey pot and carry him or her.

Hide the Thimble

This is an indoor game, great for the family, in a classroom, or at a party.

Everyone leaves the room while one person hides a thimble. The players come back in and search for it. Whoever finds it gets to hide it for the next round of play.

PUBLIC PUNISHMENT CREATED plenty of excitement in colonial towns. Criminals were put in stocks, paraded through town in chains and handcuffs, or even hanged at the gallows in front of everyone. Public hangings for burglary and murder were watched by throngs of people who came to see the event. Sometimes school was let out for the occasion, so children could watch. Public officials thought that if people saw someone punished, they wouldn't commit a crime themselves.

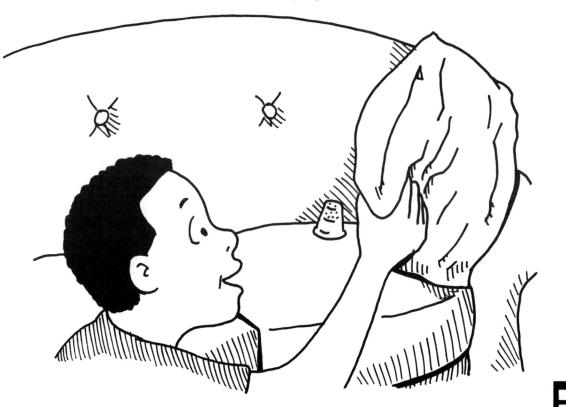

Hopscotch

In this game *you* are the game piece that moves on the board!

Play this on smooth dirt or sand, using a stick to draw the game board. If you are playing on concrete or pavement, use sidewalk chalk to draw the outline.

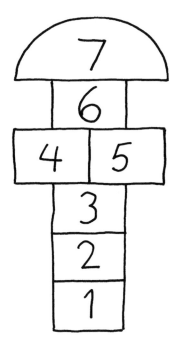

Materials

Stick or sidewalk chalk

Rocks, 1 per player

You'll need to draw 6 squares in the pattern shown and a half-circle at the end.

Each player finds a rock to toss as a place marker.

A player starts by tossing her rock into box 1 then, on 1 foot, she hops from square to square, turning around on 7 where she can place both feet on the ground. She then needs to hop back, on 1 foot, to the square just before the 1 that contains her rock. She then carefully bends down and picks up

ALL GAMES PLAYED by colonial children had to be invented and played with whatever they could find. They used their imagination to make up the games and the rules.

her rock, without stepping into the square containing it, and then jumps over this square to get to the end of the board or "home" to complete her turn.

After all players have a turn, the first player tosses her rock to the next square on the board and repeats the game but this time, she cannot hop in the new square that contains her rock.

Sound easy? If the rock rolls out of a square when it's tossed, or you use both feet in a single square, you lose your turn. You also lose your turn if you accidentally put a foot in a square that has a rock marker (yours or any other players') placed in it.

The first player to move her rock all the way to 7 and back to 1, wins!

Bilbo Catcher

One of these toys was found by archaeologists at Colonial Williamsburg, in Virginia. Colonial kids used catchers made of wood with clay balls. *Bilbo* meant sword and maybe playing with this game reminded kids of dueling with swords.

Materials

Paper cup

Sharp pencil

2 feet of string or yarn

1 2 by 1-foot piece of aluminum foil

Masking tape

Poke a hole in the side of the cup near the top with the pencil point. Pull the string through the hole and tie it in a knot. Lay the other end of the string in the center of the foil. Scrunch the foil up, crushing it into a ball shape, with the string in the middle.

Poke the pencil up through the middle of the bottom of the cup about 1 inch. Wrap tape just above and below the place where the pencil pokes through the cup to secure it.

Now, toss the foil ball up in the air and try to catch it in the cup!

Leapfrog

This is a game for four players or more and is best played outdoors.

Pick partners and designate a finish line. One person is designated as the frog. The frog crouches on the ground, while the other partner puts their hands on the frog's back and hops over him or her. Now the leaper becomes the frog, and they take turns leaping over each other, racing other teams to the finish line.

Shooting Marbles

Colonial kids sometimes made their own marbles out of clay. (You can try it with air-drying or oven-baked clays.) The prettiest marbles are made of glass, sometimes with pretty designs inside.

Marbles is an ancient game. The colonists weren't the first to play it. There's evidence that the Greeks and Romans played it, too. Marbles are one of the few toys kids had in colonial times.

Materials

1 bag of marbles
Sidewalk chalk

Draw a circle on a sidewalk. Each player puts a marble inside the circle. Players kneel outside the circle. Each player takes a turn using a *shooter* (a larger marble) to try and knock marbles out of the circle.

The shooter is a larger marble.
Flick the shooter at the marbles in the circle.

Use your thumb to flick the shooter. Try to make it hit exactly where you want it to go. You only get 1 flick per turn.

Any marbles that are knocked outside the line are won by the shooting player.

Another game of marbles is played differently. One player sets a special marble (usually a larger or fancier one) in the circle. All the other players try to roll a marble into the circle that will hit or touch the special marble. Any player's marble that misses the target loses their marble.

Everyone keeps rolling marbles at the target until someone hits it—then they win the target marble and all the other marbles in the circle!

You can imagine that marbles can be played many different ways. Make up games and rules of your own just like colonial kids did.

Horseshoe Pitching

Pitching horseshoes is fun to do outdoors using real iron horseshoes and pegs stuck in the ground. It was a game started by Roman soldiers who were the first to put shoes on their horses. Colonists played it with rings made of iron, or with rings made of rope, which they called *quoits* (say it: kwoyts).

Make a game of quoits for yourself and your friends.

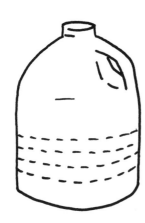

Place sand, beans, or rice in the liter bottle to keep it from tipping over.

Cut rings from a gallon jug.

THE NATIONAL HORSESHOE Pitchers Association of America holds a world championship every year.

Materials

1-liter plastic bottle
Sand, beans, or rice
1 gallon plastic jug
Scissors

Fill the liter bottle about ⅓ full with sand, beans, or rice to weight the bottom so it won't tip over easily. This will be the target.

Make rings for tossing by cutting 3 rounds from a plastic jug with scissors.

Take turns tossing the quoits at the bottle target. Keep score of how many ringers you throw that slip down over the target. A ringer is worth 3 points. If no player scores a ringer, the player with the quoit closest to the target gets 1 point. The first player to 50 points wins the game.

Try tossing the quoits from an increasing distance to challenge yourself.

Tag—You're It!

S *quat tag* is super easy and you don't need any materials to play this game, just a group of people who want to play it. Before beginning, pick a place in the play area that is called home. This is a safe area and no player can be tagged when they are in this area. One player is designated as *It*. *It* has to try to tag anybody not squatting who is outside the home area. A player is safe if they're in a squatting position—they cannot be tagged. But, since everybody has to run across the field to reach home, players can't squat down during the whole game. This is when *It* must tag the other players. The first person tagged is the new *It*.

Stone tag is another version. Players who are standing on a stone or rock are safe from *It*. You can use old magazines if you're playing indoors or don't have enough rocks.

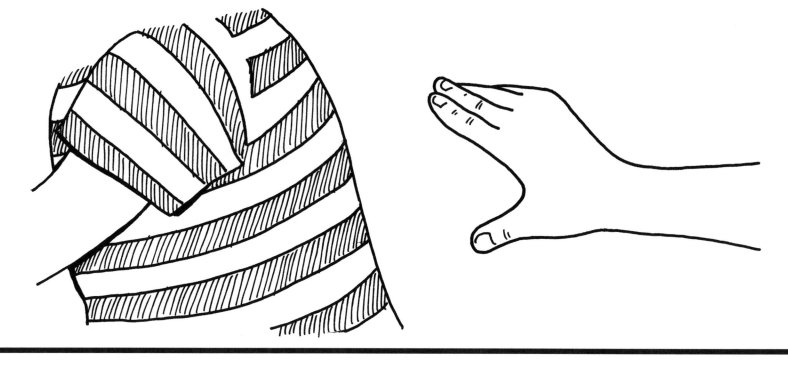

Twirl a Top

Colonial tops were carved from wood. Make a simple one from paper. Try them in different sizes—which spins faster?

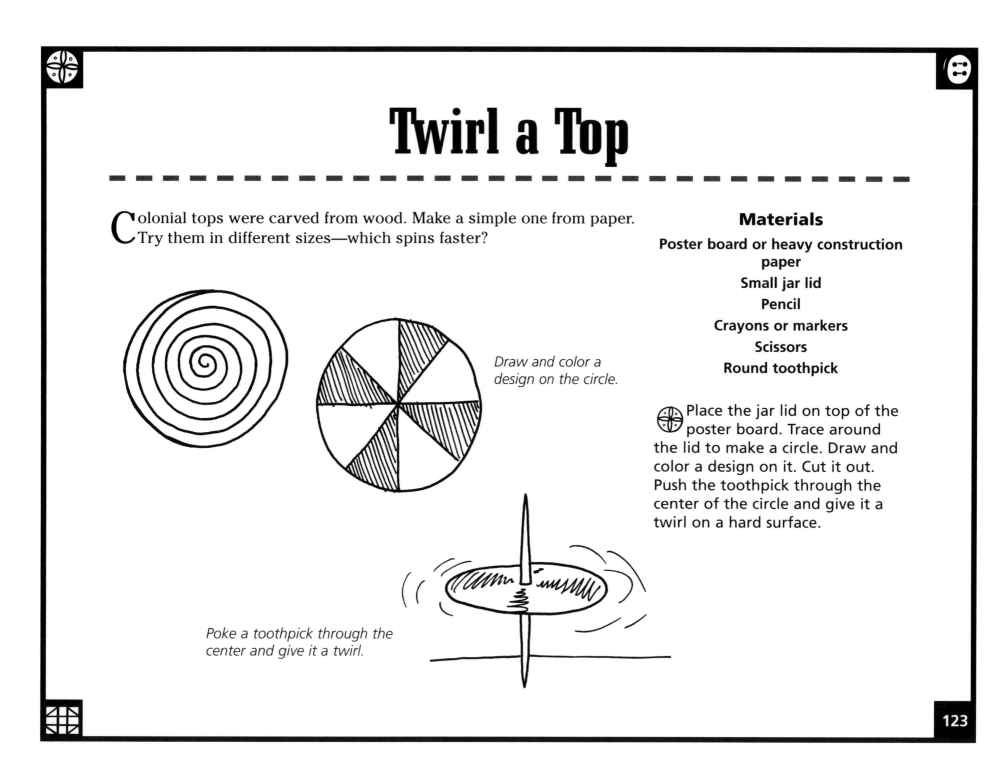

Draw and color a design on the circle.

Poke a toothpick through the center and give it a twirl.

Materials

Poster board or heavy construction paper

Small jar lid

Pencil

Crayons or markers

Scissors

Round toothpick

Place the jar lid on top of the poster board. Trace around the lid to make a circle. Draw and color a design on it. Cut it out. Push the toothpick through the center of the circle and give it a twirl on a hard surface.

Ninepins

Ninepins was also called *skittles*. Colonists from Germany and the Netherlands brought the game to North America.

You can set up a game on flat ground outdoors (that's where colonists played it).

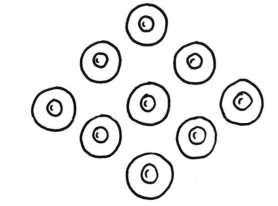

Set the pins up like this.

Materials

9 1-liter plastic bottles
Newspapers
Masking tape

Colonists used a long board to roll the ball on—it was about 1-foot wide and up to 90-feet long. If you don't have a board you can play the game without it.

Make a ball first, by wadding up newspapers and taping it to make a firm, round shape. (You can also use a ready-made ball, but, remember, colonists had to make everything!) Colonial balls were carved from wood.

Set the pins up in a diamond pattern, just like in the drawing. It's a square, with 1 corner facing you.

Mark a line to stand behind, then roll your ball toward the pins, scoring a point for every pin that topples over. Reset the pins for the next player.

Each player takes 10 turns. Whoever scores the most points, wins.

Roll the ball from behind the line.

Cornhusk Dolly

Some wealthy colonial girls had dolls shipped from England. They were made of precious porcelain, with glass eyes and human hair. Of course they were too valuable to play with, so even rich girls made simple dolls to play with everyday. Girls enjoyed making dolls from the things they found. Since everyone was growing corn, it only made sense to try to make dolls from it.

Materials

Cornhusks (available at craft stores or in the Mexican food section of your grocery store)

Heavy string or yarn

Scissors

Permanent marker

Glue

Corn silk, moss, yarn, or wool

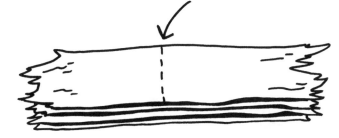

Stack, then fold 4 husks in the middle.

Lay about 4 large husks on top of each other. Fold them together in the center. Use a piece of string to tie a neck about 1-inch below the fold. That will make the head.

Roll another husk, lengthwise, to make a long tube. This will be the arms. Tie the ends, about ½ inch from the edges. That will make wrists and hands.

Slide the arm section up under the neck. Tie a string tightly below the arms to hold them in place and make a waist for the dolly.

Draw on a face with a permanent marker. Your dolly doesn't need hair, but you can add it by gluing on corn silk, moss, yarn, or wool.

If you want to make the doll wear pants, cut the bottom of the husks up to the waist tie, then tie each side about ½ inch from the bottom to make ankles and feet.

Tie a string 1 inch below the fold to make the head.

Roll 1 cornhusk and tie it at the ends to make arms and hands.

Slide the arms up to the neck.

Tie at the waist.

Spoon Doll

Colonial girls loved dolls, but they had to make them from materials they could find. Adults made dolls for children, too. Colonial dolls were made from sticks, rags, bones, pinecones—even pieces of firewood with faces drawn in soot. Dried apples, prunes, and nuts were sometimes used for heads.

Wooden dolls were the most popular. Someone would carve the wooden head, paint its eyes with charcoal and its lips and cheeks with red clay. Some doll makers were so good that they made dolls to barter or sell.

Make a little spoon doll or a whole family of them.

Materials

Small wood or plastic ice cream spoons

Markers (Permanent markers will be needed if you're using plastic spoons.)

Scraps of fabric

Rubber band

Scissors

Glue

Moss, yarn, or wool

Cut a fabric piece about 4 by 6-inches. Scrunch it around the doll's neck (the top of the spoon handle), with the skirt upside down covering the face (the spoon). Wrap the fabric in place and hold it with a tight rubber band.

Pull the fabric down over the rubber band and adjust it to be the dress.

Use the markers to draw on the doll's face and hair.

You can also glue on hair made from moss, yarn, or wool.

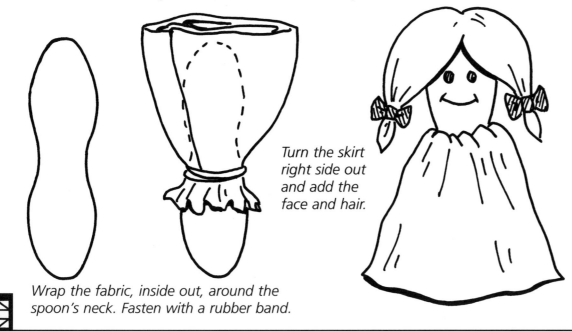

Turn the skirt right side out and add the face and hair.

Wrap the fabric, inside out, around the spoon's neck. Fasten with a rubber band.

Poppet

English children called their dolls *poppets*. You can make a poppet very easily, from an old sock. This one is a tiny baby, sound asleep.

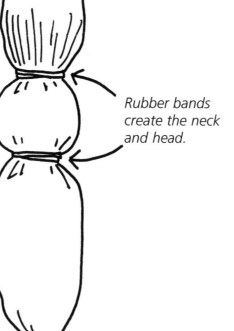

Don't stuff the cuff.

Rubber bands create the neck and head.

WOMEN SENT TO England for a *baby*, a small doll dressed in the latest clothing styles from London or Paris. They advertised in the newspaper that a *"London drest baby"* had arrived and other women could come see it for five shillings. Style-conscious ladies could sew their clothing like the doll's to keep up with the latest European fashions.

Materials

Sock
Polyester stuffing
2 rubber bands
1 12 by 12-inch piece of flannel
Needle
Thread, the same color as the sock
Scissors

Work stuffing into the sock, filling it firmly. Fasten one rubber band about ⅓-way down from the edge of the cuff. That will make the neck. Add more stuffing above the neck, and wrap another rubber band tight at the cuff. You've made the head.

Thread the needle with a double length of thread; knot at the end. Push the needle into the back of the doll's head, bringing it out where you want one of the eyes to be. Take a stitch about ½-inch long to make an eyelid. Pull it back out at the back of the head. Push the needle back into the head, coming out for the other eye. Make another ½-inch stitch for the other eyelid. Pull the needle out at the back. Pull the thread tight, so the stitches you made will bend into the shape of two closed eyelids. Knot the thread at the back of the head and cut the excess.

Turn the cuff down over the doll's head, to make a knit cap for the baby.

Wrap the baby in the piece of flannel for a blanket.

This doll is a good gift for young children, because there are no small parts they can chew off. Make as many as you have socks for—an entire nursery of sleeping poppets!

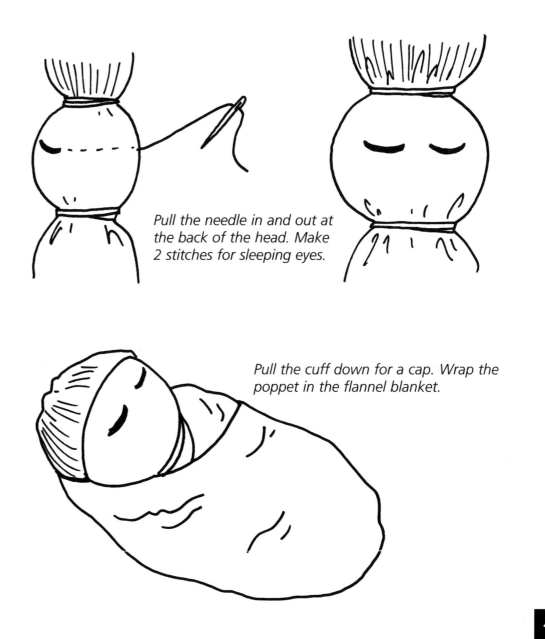

Pull the needle in and out at the back of the head. Make 2 stitches for sleeping eyes.

Pull the cuff down for a cap. Wrap the poppet in the flannel blanket.

What Happened to the Colonies?

In 1776, American colonists on the East coast joined together and fought the English in the Revolutionary War. They succeeded in sending the King of England's government back to England. Then they had the chance to form a government of their own.

They created a new nation, made up of thirteen colonies—or states—and they called this new nation the United States of America. But the union didn't stop here.

France defeated Spain in the Napoleonic Wars in Europe, and France took ownership of the Spanish territory in the New World called Louisiana (which had been owned by France in its early years). But the war had cost so much that the Emperor of France, Napoleon Bonaparte, agreed to sell the land to President Jefferson in 1803. This land became part of America, too.

The United States fought a war with Mexico between 1846-48 and won the Mexican holdings in California, Texas, Nevada, Utah, most of Arizona, and parts of New Mexico, Colorado, and Wyoming. The Mexican colonies on the West coast were taken over by hordes of miners during the California gold rush, who claimed California for the United States. The Russian colonies on the

California coast and in Alaska were abandoned when the fur trade ended.

Through the years, territories and states were added until there were fifty states. The United States of America stretched across the continent, from sea to sea, creating a country where people are guaranteed free speech, freedom of religious worship, to vote for their own leaders, and to reach their potential.

We're still a nation of immigrants, with new people coming to our country every day, hoping to make their dreams come true.

FRANCE AND ENGLAND went to war in Europe and North America in the 1750s. The English won, and the Treaty of Paris of 1763 gave all the French land in North America that lay east of the top of the Mississippi River to England. These English holdings eventually became part of Canada.

Bibliography

Beard, D. C. *The American Boys Handy Book*. Boston: David R. Godine, 1983. Reprint of 1882 edition.

Beard, Lina and Adelia Beard. *The American Girls Handy Book*. Boston: David R. Godine, 1987. Reprint of 1887 edition.

Crawford, Mary Caroline. *Social Life in Old New England*. Boston: Little, Brown & Company, 1915.

Duncan, John E. *Manners and Morals of Long Ago*. Maynard, Massachusetts: Chandler Press, 1993.

Earle, Alice Morse. *Customs and Fashions in Old New England*. New York: Charles Scribner's Sons, 1894.

Engle, Paul. *Women in the American Revolution*. Chicago: Follett Publishing Company, 1976.

Evans, Bergen, ed. *Dictionary of Quotations*. New York: Wings Books, 1969.

Hechtlinger, Adelaide. *The Seasonal Hearth: The Woman at Home in Early America*. Woodstock, New York: Overlook Press, 1986.

Jacobson, Timothy. *Discovering America: Journeys in Search of the New World*. Toronto, Ontario, Canada: Key Porter Books, 1991.

Jones, Evan. *American Food: The Gastronomic Story*. Woodstock, New York: Overlook Press, 1990.

Josselyn, John. Edited by Paul J. Lindholdt. *John Josselyn, Colonial Traveler*. Hanover, New Hampshire: University Press of New England, 1988. Reprint of 1630 original.

Simmons, Amelia. *The First American Cookbook, a Facsimile of "American Cookery, 1796"*. New York: Dover Publications, 1984.

Smith, Hervey Garrett. *The Arts of the Sailor: Knotting, Splicing, and Rope Work*. New York: Dover Publications, 1990.

Snell, Lee Toftin. *The Wild Shores, America's Beginnings*. Washington, D.C.: National Geographic Society, 1974.

Williams, Earl P., Jr. *What You Should Know About the American Flag*. Gettysburg, Pennsylvania: Thomas Publications, 1992.

Acknowledgments

Thank you to a wonderful bunch of professionals: Cynthia Sherry, Lisa Rosenthal-Hogarth, Sean O'Neill, Rita Baladad, Fran Lee, Mark Suchomel, Kathy Mirkin, Mark Voigt, Jon Updike, Missy Derkacz, and Linda and Curt Matthews. It's been a joy working on another book together!

More Books by Laurie Carlson from Chicago Review Press

Green Thumbs
A Kid's Activity Guide to Indoor and Outdoor Gardening
With a few seeds, some water and soil, and this book, kids will be creating gardens of their own in no time. "Carlson is an expert at suggesting imaginative activities. Fun, as well as educational."
    —*Skipping Stones*
ages 5–12
ISBN 1-55652-238-X
144 pages, paper, $12.95

The Days of Knights and Damsels
An Activity Guide
"This book helps you experience the era of kings, queens, and castles with more than a hundred easy projects straight out of the Middle Ages."
    —*FACES*
ages 5–12
ISBN 1-55652-227-4
184 pages, paper, $12.95

Kids Camp!
Activities for the Backyard or Wilderness
Laurie Carlson and Judith Dammel
Young campers will build an awareness of the environment, learn about insect and animal behavior, boost their self-esteem, and acquire all the basic skills for fun, successful camping.
"A good guide to outdoor adventures for inexperienced young campers and their families."
    —*School Library Journal*
ages 5–12
ISBN 1-55652-237-1
184 pages, paper, $12.95

More Than Moccasins

A Kid's Activity Guide to Traditional North American Indian Life

Kids will discover traditions and skills handed down from the people who first settled this continent.

"As an educator who works with Indian children I highly recommend [More Than Moccasins] for all kids and teachers. . . . I learned things about our Indian world I did not know."

> —Bonnie Jo Hunt
> Wicahpi Win (Star Woman)
> Standing Rock Lakota

ages 5–12
ISBN 1-55652-213-4
200 pages, paper, $12.95

Westward Ho!

An Activity Guide to the Wild West

Cowboys and cowgirls explore the West with activities such as sewing a sunbonnet, panning for gold, cooking flapjacks, singing cowboy songs, and much more.

"Crafts, recipes, songs, and games teamed with an engaging text will have young readers convinced that they're just having fun. . . . Will be heavily used by teachers in the classroom and by children at home."

> —*School Library Journal*

"Informative, well-designed, and expertly written."

> —*Children's Bookwatch*

ages 5–12
ISBN 1-55652-271-1
160 pages, paper, $12.95

Kids' Activity Books the Whole Family Can Enjoy

Big Book of Fun
Creative Learning Activities for Home and School
Carolyn Buhai Haas
Illustrated by Jane Bennet Phillips
Includes more than 200 projects and activities—from indoor-outdoor games and nature crafts to holiday ideas, cooking fun, and much more.
ages 4–12
ISBN 1-55652-020-4
288 pages, paper, $11.95

Bubble Monster
And Other Science Fun
John Falk, Robert L. Pruitt II, Kristi S. Rosenberg, and Tali A. Katz
Forty-five fun science activities created by the ScienceMinders project of the YWCA of Annapolis and Anne Arundel County.
"Eay-to-follow directions. . . . A useful purchase."
　　—*School Library Journal*
"Highly recommended."
　　—*A World of Books*
"I recommend this book for every parent."
　　—New York Hall of Science
ages 3–8
ISBN 1-55652-301-7
176 pages, paper, $17.95

Frank Lloyd Wright For Kids
Kathleen Thorne-Thomsen
A thorough biography is followed by stimulating projects that enable kids to grasp the ideas underlying Wright's work—and have fun in the process.
"Ms. Thorne-Thomsen makes learning about Wright a fun process."
　　—Meg Klinkow, Frank Lloyd Wright Home
　　and Studio Foundation
ages 8 & up
ISBN 1-55652-207-X
144 pages, paper, $14.95

Kids Celebrate!
Activities for Special Days Throughout the Year
Clare Bonfanti Braham and Maria Bonfanti Esche
Illustrations by Mary Jones
The significance of 100 different celebratory days is thoroughly explained as 200 related activities pay charming, educational tribute to the holidays, history, and accomplishments of many cultures and many people.
"Includes great illustrations and instructions for activities."
　　—*Skipping Stones*
ages 3–9
ISBN 1-55652-226-6
304 pages, paper, $14.95

Look at Me
Creative Learning Activities for Babies and Toddlers
Carolyn Buhai Haas
Illustrated by Jane Bennett Phillips
Activities for babies and toddlers that inspire creativity
and learning through play.
ISBN 1-55652-021-2
232 pages, paper, $11.95

Loaves of Fun
*A History of Bread with Activities and Recipes from Around
the World*
Beth Harbison
Illustrated by John Harbison
More than 30 recipes and activities take kids on a multi-
cultural journey to discover bread and the people who
created, cooked, ate, and enjoyed it.
"Loaves of Fun will be an adventure for kids of any age."
   —Judi Adams, President, Wheat Foods Council
ages 6–12
ISBN 1-55652-311-4
112 pages, paper, $12.95

Messy Activities and More
Virginia K. Morin
Illustrated by David Sokoloff
Foreword by Ann M. Jernberg
Encourages adults and children to have fun making a
mess with more than 160 interactive games and projects.
"Toddler-style mayhem suitable for a day care, preschool,
party, or household. . . . [Messy Activities and More] sug-
gests a number of physical and imaginative activities that
will stimulate fun for parents and small children."
   —*Booklist*
". . . family playtime that children are sure to remember
for a lifetime."
   —Toran Isom, "Growing Up Reading"
ages 3–10
ISBN 1-55652-173-1
144 pages, paper, $9.95

My Own Fun
Creative Learning Activities for Home and School
Carolyn Buhai Haas and Anita Cross Friedman
More than 160 creative learning projects and activities.
"Handy resource, includes easy-to-follow instructions for
many basic art and nature activities, science experi-
ments, and games. Recipes for such essentials as play-
dough, pastes, paints, and sidewalk chalk."
   —*Skipping Stones*
ages 7–12
ISBN 1-55652-093-X
208 pages, paper, $9.95

On Stage
Theater Games and Activities for Kids
Lisa Bany-Winters
Have fun under the footlights while playing theater games, learning about puppetry and pantomime, making sound effects, costumes, props, and scenery, applying stage makeup, and more. Several play scripts are included.
ages 6–12
ISBN 1-55652-324-6
160 pages, paper, $14.95

Sandbox Scientist
Real Science Activities for Little Kids
Michael E. Ross
Illustrated by Mary Anne Lloyd
Parents, teachers, and day-care leaders learn to assemble "Explorer kits" that will send kids off on their own investigations, in groups or individually.
"Preschool and primary-grade teachers will find this an upbeat, practical guide to science activities for young children."
　—*Booklist*
ages 2–8
ISBN 1-55652-248-7
208 pages, paper, $12.95

Shaker Children
True Stories and Crafts
Kathleen Thorne-Thomsen
This charming book combines two true biographies and authentic activities to tell children of today about the Shakers of yesterday.
"Recommended for upper elementary and middle school grade levels."
　—*School Arts*
ages 8 & up
ISBN 1-55652-250-9
128 pages, paper, $15.95

Splish Splash
Water Fun for Kids
Penny Warner
More than 120 ideas for water fun for toddlers to teens.
". . . this handy volume arms parents, teachers, and day care personnel with a wealth of great water activities for youngsters."
　—*Booklist*
ages 2–12
ISBN 1-55652-262-2
176 pages, paper, $12.95

Why Design?
Projects from the National Building Museum
Anna Slafer and Kevin Cahill
Containing photographs, illustrations, work sheets, and lists of questions for more than 40 projects, this book will stimulate anyone interested in design.
". . . this is a lively and useful paperback that uses projects to teach the value and impact of design."
 —*School Arts*
"This book is wonderful. I highly recommend it."
 —Alan Sandler, Director of Education,
  American Architectural Foundation
"This amazing book is jam-packed with ideas and information covering a multitude of subjects . . ."
 —KLIATT
ages 12 & up
ISBN 1-55652-249-5
208 pages, paper, $19.95

The Wind at Work
An Activity Guide to Windmills
Gretchen Woelfle
Including more than a dozen science activities and featuring more than 100 photos, line drawings, charts, and graphs, this book traces the history of windmills and how their design and function have changed over time.
ages 8–13
ISBN 1-55652-308-4
144 pages, paper, $14.95